The Rule of Benedict for Beginners

The Rule of Benedict for Beginners

Spirituality for Daily Life

Wil Derkse

Translated from the Dutch

by

Martin Kessler

THE LITURGICAL PRESS
Collegeville, Minnesota

www.litpress.org

To

my brothers Paul and Geert

and

my sister Marian

Cover design by David Manahan, O.S.B. Contemporary icon of Saint Benedict and Saint Scholastica by Mary Charles McGough, O.S.B., Saint Scholastica Monastery, Duluth, Minnesota.

This book was originally published in Dutch under the title *Een levensregel voor beginners: Benedictijnse spiritualiteit voor het dagelijkse leven* © Uitgeverij Lannoo nv, Tielt, 2000, The Netherlands. All rights reserved.

ISBN 13: 978-0-8146-2802-7
ISBN 10: 0-8146-2802-8

	5	6	7	8

Library of Congress Cataloging-in-Publication Data

Derkse, Wil.
    [Levensregel voor beginners. English]
    The rule of Benedict for beginners : spirituality for daily life / by Wil Derkse ; translated from the Dutch by Martin Kessler.
        p. cm.
    Includes bibliographical references.
    ISBN 0-8146-2802-8 (alk. paper)
    1. Benedict, Saint, Abbot of Monte Cassino. Regula. 2. Spiritual life—Christianity. I. Kessler, Martin, 1927– II. Title.

BX3004.Z5 D47 2003
255'.106—dc21

                                                        2002072949

Contents

Introduction

One of the blessings of the Christian life is its colorful multiplicity of spiritualities: Ignatian, Franciscan, Augustinian, Dominican, Salesian, the spirituality of Taizé, the Carmelite of Theresa of Avila and John of the Cross, Benedictine, Cistercian, and many others. These spiritualities differ considerably, both theologically and practically. But there are also important similarities. They are all related to a male or female founder—as often appears from their names—*persons* who stood at their cradle [rather than theories and concepts]. They are persons who had a great talent to listen attentively to the Spirit and who also answered from the heart as well as in practice. They all tried to incarnate this *Spirit* in a *lifestyle*. They were directed to *Christ* as their center. This centralized plurality is typically and literally *Catholic* (from the Greek: *kat'holon*], or, to express it in a more modern way: *all noses point in the same direction, but each in its different way.*

In the midst of this colorful plurality of spiritualities, the Benedictine is one of the oldest. Benedict wrote his *Rule for Monks* in the first half of the sixth century. Yet, this "handbook for quality management"—to use a contemporary word—appears suitable to offer a life orientation for thousands of nuns and monks, and at least as many laypeople. For that matter, Benedict was himself a layman, not an ordained cleric, and the communities that developed around him consisted mostly of laypeople. His *Rule* even contains two rather carefully phrased—if not discouraging—chapters about priests who might want to join the community, and about monks who are ordained deacons or priests for the sake of the community.

Among Christian spiritualities, the Benedictine is perhaps the least spectacular. It is down to earth, not dramatic, with a very modest measure of spiritual guidance, not directed toward "interesting" experiences of enlightenment or ardent moments of conversion. It is beautifully expressed in a Zen saying: "Before the enlightenment: cut wood and draw water; after the enlightenment: cut wood and draw water." This is about doing *the same thing differently*, not to ascend to totally new and different insights or mystical experiences.

Thus, Benedictine spirituality is far removed from for example the spiritual adventures in James Redfield's *De Celestijnse Belofte* [ET: The Celestine Promise]. It is firmly rooted, not swept together from all sorts of spiritual traditions; it does not make haste; it really contains nothing mysterious and esoteric; it does not target the spiritual quest of the individual, but the growth of the person who is living and imbedded in a community, with his daily and often very "worldly" activities. It is revealing that *the* central principle of Benedictine spirituality—which is not the often cited *ora et labora*, which is not even found in the *Rule* and which is even somewhat misleading because it suggests a dualism while Benedictine life wants to be "life in one piece"—is written in one of the most worldly chapters of the *Rule*: the one dealing with the manual workers of the monastery. Their products must be priced a little lower than those in "the world," not because of false competition, but in order not to give opportunity to the vice of avarice. There is also a positive reason: the sympathetic pricing serves "that God may be glorified in everything—*ut in omnibus Deus glorificetur.*" This is Benedictine spirituality in a nutshell: that *everything* offers a chance to sing God's praises—including the context of buying and selling; that *each* activity may be *sanctified*. In the most literal sense, Benedictine spirituality is *holistic*, or rather: a healing spirituality.

This book is not an introduction to Benedictine spirituality. Others have provided this and with better qualifications, namely, from the inside, living as monks or nuns.[1] I have gratefully

---

[1] See, for example, Columba Cary-Elwes, O.S.B., *Work and Prayer: The Rule of St. Benedict for Lay People*, with a new translation of the Rule by Catherine

used these sources. What I wish to attempt is to indicate how elements from this spirituality and their related lifestyle may also be fruitful outside of the walls of the monastery, to strengthen the quality of societal living and working.

On various levels and in very radically different contexts, we bear responsibility for societal living and working—as the abbot and the others do in an abbey: as (grand)parent, teacher, administrator, trainer, journalist, pastor, union leader, bishop or whatever. I have experienced that the Benedictine spirituality is a veritable treasure-trove *[Fundgrube]* of old and yet new insights which may be incarnated anew, concerning good leadership, informed decision-making, fruitful communication, good human resource management, salutary conflict resolution, a careful management of one's possessions, a blessed lifestyle which provides space. An attractive aspect is that Benedictine spirituality directs itself so distinctly toward what needs to be done here and now, at this moment. It is not directed toward remote and exalted ideals, which are only gained by spiritual masters. For her the holy is the common; her asceticism is not directed toward elevated experiences, but everyday dedication to the improvement of quality.

It would be useful if these elements could contribute something to a blessed living and working together in a more secular context. A translation into this context would be needed for that. If we should point out to coworkers in the office or shop that all of their activities are opportunities to praise God and that even their smallest acts can be sacramental and sanctifying, others might look at us puzzled and somewhat concerned—in the most favorable case, but in the most unfavorable case they might take us to the company nurse's station. If we should point out that even the smallest links in the operation of the company—even the attitude when answering the telephone— offer just as many chances for a quality-impulse, under the

---

Wybourne, o.s.b., London, 1992; also the impressive series of *Münsterschwarzacher Kleinschriften* (Vier-Türme-Verlag, Münsterschwarzach), particularly the contributions of Anselm Grün, Hein Stufkens, Gerard Mathijsen, o.s.b., *Een innerlijk avontuur. Het Benedictijner kloosterleven van binnenuit belicht*, Baarn, 1999.

motto "anything worth doing is worth doing well"—then such encouragement might be part of a realizable plan for *total quality management*. Indeed, this popular term in management jargon is in a way only the contemporary pendant of the *ut in omnibus Deus glorificetur*.

The question may naturally be asked whether principles derived from a thoroughly faithful context may simply be transferred to contexts of living and working together of those who have no direct religious orientation, of people "who do not believe"—though I would not dare claim that of anyone. The question may also be asked whether such a transfer is really "permissible," whether we do not "degrade" a thoroughly religious spirituality. I have two answers to that objection.

The first, perhaps rather frivolous, is a probably apocryphal anecdote about the great physicists Niels Bohr and Albert Einstein. Einstein visited Bohr in his summer home on the Danish coast. He noted that above the entrance, according to local usage, there was a horseshoe, supposedly to bring good luck to the dwellers of the house. "Niels," he says, "as a physicist you certainly don't believe that such a horseshoe does any good, and that it might influence the course of events?" Bohr answered: "No, of course I don't believe that, but I have heard that it also works if you do *not* believe in it."

My second answer says the same thing, but in theological dress. *Every* contribution to the cognitive, esthetic, and moral quality of this world is a contribution to the kingdom of God. When elements from Christian spirituality have a wholesome effect on the attitude and lifestyle of non-Christians or those without any Christian commitment, that should be considered gain. That is also valid when there is influencing in a "reverse" direction, for example, when elements from Buddhism, Taoism, or the environmental movement appear to be capable of being fruitful in the Christian practice of life.

However, we cannot "drag down" spirituality, and certainly not the Benedictine kind, which is expressly intended for the earth, "below," namely, to sing God's praise in *everything*.

For those who do not move in the religious channel in which Benedictine spirituality moves—but who suspect that something fruitful may be garnered from that spirituality in behalf of their own attitude and lifestyle—it may be useful to become better acquainted with the general spiritual background of Benedictine life. This is what I attempt to give in the first chapter, where I start with my own acquaintance with this lifestyle. The second chapter sketches the basic patterns of Benedictine spirituality in a more objective form in order to translate these patterns into nonmonastic contexts.

The various themes highlighted in passing (such as inspired leadership, listening decision-making, fruitfully prospering human resources, and sensible time management) will each be discussed in more detail in the following chapters.

I wish to make another remark by way of instructions for the use of this book, a remark I hardly dare to write down because it appears pedant and conceited: read *slowly* and not too much at one time. It is not intended for the rapid acquisition of information, to highlight, after a diagonal reading, some useful points with a magic-marker, or to gain a higher insight in two evenings. In the Benedictine tradition we know the *lectio divina* or spiritual reading. This entails the very slow reading of text in which one hopes to find something nurturing, until something touches you. Then you stop. What has touched you, you look at again and quietly consider inquiring as to why it touched you, what it really was and what might be your answer. It is a kind of tasting-ruminating of a text fragment, until you think that you have pretty well extracted its nourishing saps. The old monks actually called this *ruminatio,* the Latin word for what cows do with grass. Then you continue reading slowly until (hopefully) something else touches you.

I dare to write this without too much embarrassment because what will impress the reader here and there as nurturing and salutary is not original with me, but with Benedict, with the lifestyle rooted in his *Rule,* and from the contact with persons who try to live by trial and error according to the *Rule.*

I wish to emphasize living "by trial and error." Naturally, I wish to lift up in this book the beautiful, the valuable, and the fruitfulness of Benedictine life. Quite naturally, someone will react with the disillusioning remark: "But I know an abbey (or even more) where little works of all this beautiful stuff." Indeed, I do too. To begin with, in the abbey where I am a (thankful) oblate, the residents will be the first to endorse this "living by trial and error according to the *Rule*." Neither would they want to idealize their own lives. The history of abbeys has experienced times of great flourishing, but also of deep crisis. The greatest period of flourishing was perhaps the time when the community itself built its own monastery—an experience which is difficult to match. Perhaps that suggests that trying to *build* something *new* (of whatever character and no matter how modest) might be a condition for a new period of flourishing.

Presently my abbey, after spring, summer, and fall, appears to be in its winter season, though there are the first signs of spring. Such a winter season appears worse than it is. Winter is also a respectable season, in which germs are kept which quietly survive for the spring which follows, which will be different from the previous. It is like that old Irish custom which is called *grieshog*, where at the end of each day a few glowing coals are hidden under a layer of ashes. When the night is over, the coals may be uncovered to kindle a new fire.[2] To continue with this metaphor: those who would, as an outsider, meet the small and largely gray little company of abbey dwellers for the first time, might think: a lot of ashes here. But I know that there are glowing coals under the ashes. I know because each time, also in winter, I am "turned on" every time and I am certainly not the only one. There are even a few signals that the glowing coals under the ashes have ignited others to such an extent that they wish, as monks, to pass on the fire.

This book has been written in grateful solidarity with the glowing coals of the Slangenburg and those who have been ignited by them.

's-Hertogenbosch, Pentecost 2000

---

[2] I borrow this illustration from Joan Chittister, o.s.b., *The Fire in These Ashes: A Spirituality of Contemporary Religious Life*, Kansas City, 1995.

PART I

A First Acquaintance with Benedictine Spirituality[1]

1. *A Lesson from the Imagery of Hildegard's Abbey in Eibingen*

According to Benedict, the abbot needs to clarify what is good and salutary by his deeds rather than by his words. The Feijenoord club[2] motto *Geen woorden maar daden* [No words but deeds] apparently has a Benedictine background. The abbot must teach by his example rather than by long-winded speeches.

Also, to get acquainted with Benedictine spirituality, examples can say more than words. In 1980 the KRO[3] produced two brilliant TV series about the monastic life. They have been published as video's under the titles *Abdijen van de lage landen* [Abbeys of the Low Countries] and *Abdijen van Europa* [Abbeys of Europe].[4]

---

[1] For a beautiful description of Benedictine life see Kathleen Norris, *The Cloister Walk*, New York: Riverhead Books, 1996.

[2] This is the name of the Rotterdam Soccer Club.

[3] Dutch Catholic Radio.

[4] These two series have also been published as books: Michel van der Plas, *Abdijen in de lage landen, en de mensen die er wonen*, with photography by Robin Lutz, Tielt/Baarn, 1989; Ton van Schaik, *Abdijen in West-Europa en hun bewoners*, with photography by Robin Lutz, Tielt/Baarn, 1992. To remind myself now and then as to what monastic life is about, I only need to consult some of Robin Lutz's photos to impress me again.

As you might expect, in the first series I was particularly impressed by the portrait of my abbey, the St. Willibrord Abbey in Doetinchem-Slangenburg, in the Netherlands. I have become increasingly committed to this abbey. The commentary by Abbot Van den Biesen on the familiar statuary is down to earth: the fact that they built the abbey themselves, has thoroughly determined the *spirit* of this community, though it is hardly spectacular in a visible sense.

But for a first acquaintance with the content of Benedictine life I would rather recommend an episode from the second series, namely, the one illustrating the daily life of the nuns which inhabit the Hildegard Abbey in the German village of Eibingen, near the ruins of the abbey which was built in the twelfth century by the multitalented Benedictine, Hildegard of Bingen.

The image which this abbey suggests tends to impress many as strange and alienating. What motivates a group of almost sixty women of three generations to live under the authority of an abbess, guided by an about 1500-year-old *Rule* for monks? "What are you doing there in the Middle Ages?" might be an understandable question. But little details quickly show that these women very much live in the present time: a GPS system clipped to their habit, modern kitchen utensils, computers, modern wine glasses—all have their place in the abbey. We see the nuns during the different moments of their daily rhythm: singing the praises of God (in beautifully polished Gregorian) in the cloister church, their work: the careful activity of the goldsmith, the thorough cleaning of the lamp shades in the chapel, a careful *privatissimum* on phenomenology by the abbess (a philosopher with a doctor's degree) to a young novice, arranging flowers for the altar, activities in the wine cellars, with an attentive private lecture in their own room, a telephone conversation in the ambulatory where the nun takes a seat in the niche to give the caller proper attention, the laying of new electrical cables during the recreation period . . .

When we concentrate for some time on these images, three things attract our attention. First, that with all of these activities, the sisters are striving to pay *attention* to anything whatever—including recreation; everything is done in a spirit of attentive cultivation. Whenever I watch this video I have to think about the simple rule of the novelist Iris Murdoch who summarizes in a nutshell the principle of a good life: *to attend and get things right*—to pay attention that things may be in order, that is what it always amounts to.

A second characteristic which the viewer will notice is the calm *beauty* and properly maintained *order* of the abbey, including the kitchen and the other work places. That is also the case when there are no TV cameras present. Abbeys breathe a spirit of care and culture, a radiation to which little things also contribute: some nicely arranged flowers, carefully cleaned and arranged tools, the precise handwriting in which the comments of the philosophiles are noted. Little things which are *important*. Beauty and order are contagious in their effect. A student once showed me a small but convincing proof of that. He showed me his note pad on which he had written the college notes of the previous week. Most notes had apparently been made in haste, much was arranged topsy-turvy and the legibility left something to be desired. But there was a notable exception: a college handout. This particular professor made writing an art; he wrote everything very neatly and beautifully, in ordered sequence and in a beautiful, legible handwriting. His college notes are therefore not produced by a word processor but in handwriting—a habit which meanwhile has been adopted by many colleagues of the department. Without the student making a considered decision on this, the notes of *this* course were organized, written beautifully, very legibly—an orchid among the weeds. Order and beauty are contagious. So are disorder and ugliness. That is the case with little things such as the keeping up to date of a note pad, but also with the running of a large company or of a ministerium.

Monastic life radiates; in its limited context but often also in the history of culture and ideas: first religiously and spiritually, but also artistically, intellectually, socially, and economically. Abbeys have brought *culture* to Europe (and not only to Europe). That is a historical fact of major significance. Approaching the vicinity of *living* monastic communities one can see in the landscape that there is a relationship to the source of quality. For example, there are a notable number of butterflies in the vicinity of Egmond (the Netherlands). Ask the Benedictines in that area: one of the brothers cultivates a butterfly garden.

This radiation is also less directly noticeable: an abbey is surrounded by a circle of people and activities which are fed by the monastic life. In some countries like Germany, England, and the United States, some Benedictine abbeys have high ranking high schools or universities noted for their quality. Others publish theological, philosophical, liturgical, or general-cultural journals to which many contribute who are not monks and nuns. Others again concentrate on the arts and the study and cultivation of Gregorian chant. Additionally, there are many regular and irregular guests: people who withdraw for study but also wish to get in touch with something else (see below), people who choose a week of reflection before beginning a new position, people who have been hurt or confused and find an ordered and wholesome atmosphere in an abbey.

More recently, a new offshoot has been added to such a radiation, namely, presence on the Internet. The websites of dozens of abbeys draw many visitors, sometimes thousands a day.[5] The often beautifully executed homepages provide links to spiritual texts, beautiful music, a virtual tour through the abbey, acquaintance with the daily schedule and its spiritual background, or the ordering of books.

These many facets are an informative lesson for other institutions. Schools, universities, and commercial organizations might in similar ways cultivate their direct and indirect environment, intellectually, artistically, socially, and economically.

*   *   *

Back to the images of the Hildegard Abbey. There is a third notable characteristic related to the previous two; one sees and clearly senses that the one activity (for example, making jewelry) does not receive more attention and care than others (for example, cleaning lamp shades). A private lecture in phenomenology is not more "important" than arranging flowers

---

[5] An example is <www.osb.org>, provided by St. John's Abbey, Collegeville, Minnesota, which has other links for surfing.

in the chapel. A telephone conversation cannot be handled any more carelessly than the laying of electrical wires or the singing of psalms.

Already on first acquaintance we gain the insight that there is no sharp division between the sacred and the profane in an abbey. Benedict's *Rule for Monasteries* inspires this attitude. That may be illustrated, for example, in chapter 31 about the cellarer (in effect, the economist and material manager) of the monastery, where we read: "Let him regard all the utensils of the monastery and its whole property as if they were the sacred vessels of the altar." Also, relating to the *attitude* of the monks in their diverse daily activities, there is a continuing line. A wise abbot gave the following advice to some novices who did not know how solemnly they should walk: "In chapel you should comport yourself as you do during recreation: relaxed. During recreation, you should comport yourself as you do in chapel: with dignity."

The characteristics which are signaled in the Abbey of Hildegard are equally valid as little lessons which may be applied in the contexts of our lives and which might raise the quality of life. The cultivation of an attentive attitude—whoever may ask for our attention—is just as important in the life of the family as in a teaching situation, with the repair of a bicycle tire as well as the writing of a learned article, when you participate in the liturgy or when involved in a late night conversation with a good friend. Sharing a fine bottle of wine, tasting it attentively, or listening carefully in a conversation and giving a suitable response, are in a certain sense just as sacramental as going to Communion.

This is related to the second lesson: that tasks and activities may indeed differ in weight, but the one is not worthy of more attention (is "more sacred") than the other. This attitude is especially difficult to cultivate. It is very tempting and quite natural to view some activities as more worthy of our time and attention than others: the writing of an important executive notice, the preparation for a crucial meeting with a generous philanthropist, the writing of a keynote lecture for an international scientific congress, or the composing of a report for a meeting of bishops. But we might be tempted to consider other activities less important, such as the following: repairing your daughter's bicycle tire, the recreational reading of a bedtime story to a child, or the careful scrubbing of your kitchen floor. But when we realize that all of these tasks, though not the same, are equally worthy, and that all of them deserve to be done attentively, as opportunities "to praise God," or, in a more secular vein, *to attend and get things right,* and when we respond to this awareness, then all activities will increase in quality. By scrubbing the floor well when that needs to be done, the writing of that keynote lecture gains in quality when that is on my daily schedule as well.

The examples just referred to are derived from my personal life, in which I realize all too well how great may be the distance between the ideal which Benedict's *Rule* holds before me and how well I manage in my daily life. Meanwhile, I know that it is no different for monks and nuns. Fortunately, Benedict writes very reassuringly that this is a rule for beginners. He does not mean by that, that after reading it and after sufficient practice we are promoted to the following level, while he offers another rule for the more advanced. To the contrary: there is *only* this rule for beginners. We *remain* always and daily beginners on our pilgrim road to a better quality of life. In that sense, the monk or the nun, who already made their professions sixty years ago, remain novices. As an old abbot once said when he was asked by a journalist what more than a half a century of Benedictine life amounted to: "Falling and getting up again. Falling and getting up again." It is no different outside the monastery.

A rule for beginners. There is no higher level on which spiritual professions should move. Again, we see a difference here, for example, with the spiritual adventures in *The Celestine Promise,* where the leading persons are led in rapid tempo from the first insight to the second, from the second to the third, etc., and in sequence, eventually reach the tenth insight. With Benedict there is only one level: the level of the beginner, and there is only a slow tempo: the level of the beginner: the one from day to day where we practice *piecemeal spiritual improvement management,* what is called in Latin *conversatio morum* (one of the three vows which the monk makes). Others may find that disappointing; personally, I find this a very hopeful and comforting thought that Benedictine life is not intended for spiritual musclemen.

2. *What I Learned through My Own Acquaintance with Benedictine Life*

My own process of trial and error during the past eighteen years has gradually more and more been determined by this "rule for beginners," and by an increasingly shrinking and rather inauspicious little group of mostly older men who try to live as a community according to this rule: the monks of the modest but beautiful St. Willibrord's Abbey in Doetinchem-Slangenburg, in the Netherlands. First, I came as a regular guest, but felt gradually more at home in this community until at a certain moment I responded to the invitation to associate myself with the community as a layman, to become an *oblate.*

I take the liberty to devote a few pages to this development because from this process of (exceptionally modest) personal growth something may be learned about the basic patterns of Benedictine spirituality and about its (exceptionally modest) fruits.

The first time I came as a guest to the abbey was December 1982. My younger brother, who had been there more often and had even thought about entering, had invited me to accompany him on his annual visit. I had just begun with a new study, and would be able to work there quietly. It surely was quiet. I worked on my paper constantly, and more out of politeness toward my hosts than from great religious zeal six times a day I stood with them in the little abbey church. I felt rather uncomfortable there. These services, called "Hours," appeared to me for the most part remarkably unproductive, without any form or "outcome" as in the liturgy I knew from elsewhere: the Eucharist which leads to a communal rite, baptism, the celebration of marriage, the funeral, confirmation.

Psalms, antiphons, songs and hymns were sung, apparently according to a system, which seemed more complicated to me than the irreversible theory of thermodynamics. There was a reading, followed by a silence which appeared irritatingly long (it was less than five minutes, but that is a lot of silence for a busy, restless fellow), a prayer, and a sung acclamation. After that, neatly leaving the church in procession. With the candles extinguished, there was not a single result, except that the praise of God was sung. As if he needed that, was my irreverent thought—but moreover incorrectly, as I learned later: *we* need it.

With the series of psalms in each of the Hours I felt particularly uncomfortable during the close of each psalm: "Glory to the Father, the Son, and the Holy Spirit . . . ," at which one made a bow. I found it difficult to bow with them and the enthusiastic bowing by some other guests disturbed me, who undoubtedly wanted to make me understand how familiar they were with the ritual in this place. I find it a slightly disturbing thought that present newcomers are possibly just as disturbed by my bowing.

The only hour which I enjoyed from the first day was the close of the day or Compline, whereby the day of singing, praying, reading, working, and recreating is completed, after which follows the silence of the night. It is a pleasant and simple service: quietly searching the conscience, confession of sin (which sins?, I asked naively), the same three psalms every night, the texts of which for once were immediately clear to me (Psalm 4; Psalm 91: God's protection; Psalm 134: prayer for a blessing), Song of Simeon ("Lord, let your servant go in peace . . . "), a brief prayer, and a blessing with holy water by the abbot or prior. Then all the lights are extinguished, with the exception of a little spot on the statue of Mary, high in a niche, and a Gregorian Hymn of Mary is sung. This remarkable moment touched me immediately. What a strange situation: fourteen adult men, none on the surface seriously spiritually disturbed, who sang a very old song in the dark, their eyes directed to a lifeless statue. They do this every evening, year after year. What is going on here? I was moved, and was momentarily no longer sure that I came here only to study.

During the first week I learned three more things. Gradually, I had less of a problem with bowing at the "Glory to the Father . . ."; it fit well with the words which indicated the Threefold Most High. Benedictine spirituality is partly a way of life of simply learning to join, a spirituality which shows examples for others to follow. Only in a limited sense is there a question of "spiritual guidance" in an abbey. The guests may speak to a guest priest if they want, but a guest priest is not very apt to initiate a "spiritual conversation" on his own. Postulants and novices are, in conversation with the novice master, introduced to certain aspects of Benedictine spirituality and attitude, but most things they probably gather by simply joining and watching others. That is what happened to me with bowing which was difficult at first: externally joining a little with the monastic custom can gradually change your inner attitude and response, so that external joining comes easier. When I now quietly read a psalm on the train, I sometimes have to suppress the inclination to stand at the end and to bow—for someone might warn the train personnel.

The second thing I learned, at the time just superficially, concerned the blessings of the Benedictine dealing with time. I will return to this topic. The rhythm of time for choral prayer, work, meals, and recreation had a salutary effect on my general well-being and proved to be surprisingly efficient in my own work. I wrote more pages per day during the free limited number of working hours (four or six) in the abbey than during a full day at home, dedicated to study. Not only because I had less interruptions, but also because of "simply joining in" which I mentioned earlier. The clock regulating the division of the day had to be obeyed anyhow—an obedience which can be remarkably liberating. The clock indicates that the choral prayer begins in ten minutes, *so* the monk (and often the guest as well) shuts off his mower, puts down his pen or closes his book, and walks to the monastery church with his choral book—a lesson in the art of quitting. The clock indicates the end of recreation time and *so* you pick up your pen and book again, start the motor of the mower or begin to scrub the floor—a lesson in the art of beginning. To an outsider this may appear quite brave and artificial, but by joining such a daily rhythm and to get some practice in both the art of beginning (how easily we put that off) and in the art of quitting (very important in a dangerously overloaded society), you work both more effectively and more relaxed; such is my experience. Certainly when one adopts the habit to give every part of the daily scheme its own value: not thinking ahead about your keynote lecture while you scrub the floor, or grumbling a bit about your colleague's wrong remarks earlier that day.

In the beginning I needed to get used to the fact that recreation also has its own value in the daily rhythm. Recreation also deserves to be cultivated. During the afternoon washing of dishes on one of my first days in the monastery I announced eagerly: "And now, next I go back to my paper on Aristotle!" "Never mind Aristotle," said the guest priest acting firmly (but really he was serious), "now is recreation. Join me for a walk?" A bit irritated by this apparent blind obedience to the monastic daily scheme I followed him. Forty-five minutes later, when the clock had given the signal, I sat at the desk, my mind reasonably refreshed.

The third lesson of this first week: the importance of a simple but effective care for little things in your environment. One of the monks, Father Schretlen, a beloved father confessor and conversation partner for many people, was also the custodian of the monastic church. One of his functions was the care of the flowers in the chapel and elsewhere in the monastery. He was often seen paying attention to aspects of this task: removing a few wilted leaves, cleaning up some fallen leaves of trees, rearranging a bouquet, replacing a candle, straightening out a few chairs. This was not at all an obsession or a sign of obsessive-compulsive neurosis. Father Schretlen simply was careful in noting little things in his area which needed a bit of attention.

Since I try to keep my own (strongly modified) version of a daily order which I have copied from the abbey, my daily scheme also contains an FSE, that means the "Father Schretlen effect." That simply means that every day I at least keep in mind how I might follow his example, at home, at work, and wherever I am: replacing a broken light bulb, filling the water containers of the radiators, turning off the reading light when I leave the train compartment. I know that this hardly represents anything, yet I am ashamed at nighttime when I notice that I did not mark off my FSE.

3. *Growing toward the Oblature*

These are a few lessons, vaguely absorbed during my first visit to the abbey. More followed later, so that I gradually came not only to work quietly. Very gradually my orientation changed. In this first phase I became more and more "interested" in the Benedictine life and spirituality, because I noticed that it did me good. I began reading the *Rule* of Benedict, which at first largely disappointed me, but whose value for my own life orientation, thanks to good commentaries, gradually became clear to me.

A dangerous and very un-Benedictine phase followed in which I, working and living "in the world" began to long intensely and passionately for my visits to the abbey, as an escape from my increased tasks and responsibilities, as a safe haven, as an institute for spiritual intensive care where I might be connected to the infusion tube for a few days. I sometimes thought, if I had known this Benedictine world earlier, I would not have chosen marriage and public active life. I call this "un-Benedictine" because Benedict is not interested in "running away" from something to which you have committed yourself.

Thanks to the careful rereading of the *Rule* and its interpretations by Esther de Waal, Columba Cary-Elwes, and Anselm Grün, and particularly by brief conversations with and casual remarks by monks and by my brother in the kitchen washing dishes, and in the woods of the abbey, I gained another view of what Benedictine spirituality might mean for me. There was a change on two tracks: from "being interested in" to "being committed to" a Benedictine lifestyle; from the feeling "it does me good" to the call to lead a life, from the inspiration "that it might do me good," not in my monastic refuge, but in my everyday context of family, work, and social life.

This additional, unspectacular development was apparently noticed, for the monastic community invited me and a few others (my brother among them) to associate ourselves with the abbey as laymen, to become *oblates*. After a preparatory year we made our "oblate profession" at the altar of the chapel during a celebration of the Eucharist and placed our signed "oblate promises" in the hands of the one who would also be our abbot.

To be an oblate simply means: to orient yourself, from a distance, to the monastic life of the community to which you have bound yourself. Additionally, oblates and the monastic community mutually try to be of service. Such orientation to the monastic life consists of three main aspects (just like the life of monks and nuns): choral prayer or office (for oblates naturally in a modified form), doing your work of all kinds in a Benedictine manner, and the daily "prayerful reading" *(lectio divina)* of spiritual texts (among them, the *Rule*). The daily life of the oblate is also based on three monastic promises:

- *stabilitas* (meaning: do not walk away from what you have committed yourself to, and which makes an appeal to you here and now);

- *conversatio morum* (meaning: the process of being engaged in permanently and daily to improve your attitude and lifestyle); and

- *obedientia* (meaning: the art of careful listening and responding from the heart and actively).

For those who have bound themselves as monk, nun, or oblate to the Benedictine life, it is a daily experience that this form of spirituality cannot be possessed or "had" (like a first, second, or even tenth insight in *The Celestine Promise*), but that it offers a number of quality perspectives on which one needs to work every day.

Precisely against this everyday background, these perspectives and orientations may also be inspiring and fruitful in contexts other than life in the abbey, such as in the family, at work, in social life, and in school. In these contexts are also needed *piecemeal management for improvement,* careful listening to what people and situations demand of you, and to reply, and not walking away from what you have committed yourself to—rather than spectacular total changes or revolutions normally accomplished by spiritual giants and supermen.

PART II

Basic Patterns of Benedictine Spirituality and First Translation to Nonmonastic Contexts[1]

1. *The Benedictine Way of Life: Listening Attentively to Gain Results*

RULE

For many, the word "rule" primarily conveys a normative, limiting, even a negative sound. The expression "keeping to the rules" reminds us of what is not allowed at all, where *limits* are faced that may not be crossed and where stipulated sanctions follow the transgression of the rules.

In the *Rule* of Benedict there are these elements, but they always serve *positive* values: personal growth, the prospering of the community, taking good care of things. Even the prescriptions regulating correcting and punitive actions of the abbot are targeted toward welfare and improvement, not toward revenge or punishment as such. Rules and norms should always be seen as giving support on a road which leads toward positive values. Things are regulated in view of a goal, a value to be

---

[1] I am grateful for Esther de Waals, *A Life-Giving Way: A Commentary on the Rule of St. Benedict,* London, 1995, and for her earlier books: *Seeking God: The Way of St. Benedict,* London, 1984, and *Living with Contradiction: Further Reflections on the Rule,* London, 1988.

achieved. When the connection between rule and value is missing, a rule is worthless. Rules and norms which are devoid of values are empty and are therefore not respected.

When norms of whatever kind are blurred in a family, a business, a societal organization, or in a community, there is something wrong with the communication of values. Mostly, people know the rules quite well, but they do not grasp their rationale, neither do they share any longer the value context from which rules and norms may be understood intelligently. *On the other hand, situations arise whereby those rules hardly need to be pointed out precisely because of a positive communication of values; on a microlevel this would refer to exemplary behavior, where commitment to a value context is desired.* Musicians in an orchestra study much harder for an inspiring conductor, even beyond what may be required by a *labor agreement;* a teacher who functions well seldom if ever needs to punish students or dismiss them; with an entrepreneur who has his heart in the business and who cares for his people (which is the same thing), absenteeism of his workers is demonstrably lower than average.

The Benedictine rule of life is therefore not a monastic law book of criminal law, but a guide in the school of life. It is not a rigid code, but a balanced program for *becoming human* and for *the incarnation of values.* Consider in this connection Martin Buber's "Germanized" rendering of the Hebrew word *Torah* in the Scriptures: it is not a *Gesetz* [law] (no joy is to be found in that, it does not make one dance) but *Weisung* [instruction]: a tested salutary and fruitful help with your life orientation. Jewish tradition has a festival of the Joy of the Torah, where there is dancing with the Torah scrolls. That would hardly ever happen in a judicial court.

In the *Rule* of Benedict the joining of order and flexibility is noteworthy. I find it almost humorous that Benedict has dedicated long chapters toward an orderly regulation of even the smallest details of the divisions of the psalms for the different Hours, but then writes: "if this distribution of the Psalms is displeasing to anyone, he should arrange them otherwise, in whatever way he considers better . . ." (ch. 18)—provided that the substitute list be orderly arranged. That is typically Benedictine: order and regularity are essential for a blessed life, provided they are combined with flexibility.

LISTENING AND RESPONDING

In the abbey, there is daily reading from the *Rule* of Benedict and I try to do it at home as well. There are many definitely practical chapters—about clothing and shoes, about what psalms must be sung and when, about correction and punishment. Only with regular rumination *[preoccupation]* aided by experienced commentators can these passages be spiritually nurturing. Other parts of the *Rule* speak to us when read quietly and reflected upon, like the Prologue, the chapters concerning the abbot and the cellarer (the "economist"), as well as the short chapter about the manner in which decisions are to be made in the monastery.

The first sentence of the Prologue contains the entire Benedictine life program in a nutshell: "Listen, my son, to your master's precepts, and incline the ear of your heart. Receive willingly and carry out effectively your loving father's advice, that by the labor of obedience you may return to Him from whom you had departed by the sloth of disobedience." This is not a severe and dominating commander speaking, but a loving master and father. Also, this is not about blind obedience or the discipline of a slave: the master and father hope for a hearty and willing agreement and an active carrying out of his rules.

"Listen," the first word of the *Rule*, has a special sound. Latin uses here *obsculta* or *ausculta:* it means listening very attentively, as when a doctor "auscultates" ["listens"] to a patient with a stethoscope. The goal of such attentive listening is to hear what the situation demands of us, and then to respond to it. Benedictine life may be summarized in a single rule: to listen very carefully and to respond heartily and actively, not out of free-floating courage, but to achieve a *result*. To put it theologically: the word which has been heard must become incarnate, transformed into reality, into results.

The last word of the Rule is *pervenies:* we arrive where we want to be, we achieve a result. Benedictine life is: to listen carefully to *achieve* a result. This is an attitude which, of course, may also be cultivated outside of the monastery.

From this attitude of attentive listening (and other forms of careful attention) to achieve a good result, a few simple, obvious lessons may be learned.

May we speak of a bad result? In that case, we have often paid insufficient attention. This is the case with small things, but also with far less innocent matters. The repaired bicycle tire is leaking again? We did not carefully check the rim and the outer tire for protruding spokes or remaining sharp objects; we did not pay attention to the *patching;* we did not take sufficient care replacing the tire with the clamps so that we made a hole. A Boeing 747 crashed in the Bijlmer (southeast of Amsterdam). The engine connecting pins had been inspected with insufficient care; it was not noticed that one of the engines was unbalanced, or perhaps it was noticed but assumed that it would be sorted out in Tel Aviv the next morning; carelessness in the communication between crew and traffic personnel. Much of what goes wrong, both small and not so small, is not the result of negative intentions or evil plans, but of bad listening, carelessness, sloppy work, and bungling. And vice versa: where something succeeds notably well (an ice-breaking opening in a negotiation, to a dazzling performance of Shostakovich's *Fifth Symphony* and the safe piloting of a heavily damaged airplane), that may often be related to the ability to listen well to one another, with full attention, on the edge of your chair as it were, with all antennas extended.

THE BENEDICTINE VIEW OF HUMANITY:
WE ARE ABLE TO KEEP GROWING

The Benedictine series of careful listening, to agree heartily, and to achieve results, illustrates a view of humanity and a psychology that presupposes the experience of a person who pays attention and responds, who has great talents for spiritual growth. In this, I take the term "spiritual" very broadly in the sense of everything that has to do with the "life of the spirit," including, for example, making music and having a good conversation with friends.

That being human is not a condition but a charge, containing a growth process, is an insight common to all times. Some time ago, I read with my students at the Technical University at Eindhoven (the Netherlands) a text from the personal notes of the Roman emperor Marcus Aurelius. This passage from his second-century diary sounded quite familiar to my students (and myself):

> When you arise reluctantly early in the morning, think like this: I arise to accomplish a human task. Should I then complain, when I am about to do that for which I was born, and for which I was placed on earth? Or was I created to pamper myself under the blankets, even if that is more pleasant. Were you born, then, to enjoy and, generally to feel, but not to *act*? Don't you see the plants, the birds, the ants, the spiders, the bees, who all perform their own tasks and in their own way, helping to let the cosmos function? Don't you then want to do your work as a human? Don't you hasten to do what is befitting with *your* nature?[2]

What then is our nature, our disposition? What is specifically human? Can we say something intelligent about that? To begin with, we may affirm that human beings—differently from birds, ants, spiders, and bees—when we are physically full-grown, we are not altogether *complete*. Even at an advanced age people may yet have the gnawing feeling that they need to change drastically, that they need to *work* on themselves, though they are not quite sure how to do so. In many functions we have a noticeable potential for *growth*. A mature hunting leopard can reach a top speed of a little over 100 km per hour. We would be greatly surprised if a more experienced hunting leopard would exceed a speed faster than 1000 km per hour. But that is the case with us in certain functions. Children are placed in a junior high-school class and (most of them) know how to add and to turn on a gas flame. After their final exams they (most of them) know how to partly specialize, to operate a chromatograph or understand the mechanism of nuclear aromatic substitution. Give an untrained person a violin and a

[2] This quote is translated from Marcus Aurelius, *Persoonlijke notities.* Baarn, 1994, 91.

bow and the sound is unbearable to listen to, but after putting his heart in it with a diligent *commitment* that person may eventually play Brahms's violin concerto.

As in the case of the authentic life as a hunting leopard, a number of vital conditions and functions may be determined (for the leopard: developing high speed, not being frightened away at the sight of an antelope, etc.), so we could name certain vital and spiritual conditions which pertain to every authentic human being. This has been done quite pointedly (and in a way that it is easy to remember) by Canadian philosopher Bernard Lonergan, S.J., who formulated five "transcendental imperatives" for authentic human life;[3] Benedict would have nodded his approval. We do not need to be taken aback by these terms: they are called "transcendental" because they are valid for *everyone, everywhere,* and *always,* and they are called "imperatives" because we need to *work* on them. They are charges—that is why they are all followed by exclamation marks:

- *Be attentive!* Pay attention, be alert, listen carefully to what is happening—and not only to what suits you. Listen to what the situation and the other person demands of you, like the physician with the stethoscope who listens for breathing and for the heartbeat of a patient—what is going on? What needs to be done?

- *Be intelligent!* Attempt to *read* the result of your paying attention (*intellectus* is sometimes related with *intus legere*: reading toward the inside), introduce order and structure and try to grasp it.

- *Be reasonable!* Be sensible. Weigh the products of your understanding, try to arrive at a good judgment. To be sensible is something else from being intelligent, however. For example, it is intelligent to grasp the fact that lowering the cost can positively influence the bottom line of your business. But it is sensible, if not clever, to see, after close consideration, that the raising of the cost (investing) as part of a good strategy

---

[3] Bernard Lonergan, S.J., *Method in Theology*. Toronto, 1996, fifth printing.

may influence the bottom line still more positively (because it may be more permanent).

- *Be responsible!* Be responsible, realize the gradations in moral quality of your thoughts and actions and be approachable on this, respond in a practical manner to what the situation or the other person expects of you.

- *Be in love!* Put your heart into something, give your "yes," be committed, try to give a hearty response, be dedicated.

These functions go together, simultaneously, not successively: after or beside each other. With the proper repair of a leaking bicycle tire, by the good solution of a mathematical problem, with a pleasant conversation with friends, during a staff meeting, with the choosing of a new bishop, when I speak with someone during a reception: with all of these, these five functions may be cultivated simultaneously. It would be odd to say: on the factory floor they only pay attention and understand, middle management is involved in choosing sensibly and responsibly, while putting their heart into something pertains to the management council.

Lonergan's five functions may be practiced always and every place where people live and work together: in an abbey, in school, in a business, in a hospital. In all of these places these rules are valid: to educate properly, to train and to exercise leadership is to stimulate and exercise sensitivity toward paying attention, understanding, choosing sensibly and falling in love, so that people may continue to grow and broaden their horizon. That is not one-way traffic. Many a teacher is taught by his pupils, many a father is corrected by one of his children, many a manager learned commitment to his business by noting it in one of his workers.

Lonergan's imperatives naturally and quite clearly implicate a human vision. The human is a being with a permanent capacity for growth which is never finished, always capable of exceeding earlier cognitive, esthetic, and moral limits. This constant being on the road (formerly it was called man as *homo viator*, man as a traveler), this realization that we daily need to work on our growth, fits seamlessly with the human vision of

Benedict. The monk also remains a permanent student, a beginner, a careful listener to what every new situation demands of him. The three monastic vows by which he seals his commitment to monastic life are therefore not seen as the conclusion of his training, but as formulations of these rules of quality which he needs to keep daily before him, in his eyes and in his ears.

2. *The Benedictine Vows:*
Directed toward Growth and Liberation

As a boy I learned that there were three monastic vows: obedience, poverty, and chastity. As I remember, they were mostly portrayed to us as negative and limiting. When taking vows, one had to give up things in three areas which are important to nonmonastics: not doing what you wanted (giving up your freedom), not being able to control things which make life pleasant (giving up possessions), and not making love (giving up physical intimacy with others). As we were told more implicitly than explicitly, this last vow might well be the most difficult of all.

To be a religious was therefore a matter of giving up things, and the more difficult it was, the more valuable it would be. It was about curtailing your natural longings. One made his life "narrower" in many respects (some religious pictures showed a narrow gate to salvation, while the road to damnation was pleasantly roomy) and poorer; you enclosed yourself behind high walls. One only needed to add barbed wire and watchtowers to make it look like a prison.

This image has been very harmful, and moreover in many respects a distortion of Benedict's intentions. To begin with, the series of monastic vows is quite different: *stabilitas, conversatio* (or *conversio*) *morum,* and *obedientia,* to be translated as: stability, daily improvement of attitude and lifestyle, and listening attentively and from the heart to what the abbot, brothers, and others ask of you. Moreover, they are expressly targeted toward growth and liberation, not curtailing and narrowing. The rules which flow from this are *in the service of* growth and liberation.

Thus, it stands to reason that good communal living *together* of people in a monastic *community* is not helped by intimate cliques (which creates bad results), or by selfishly claiming everything for oneself, or by divisive decision-making that is unregulated and only directed to particular interests. From this stems the interest in chastity, being without possessions, and obedience. But that does not imply rejection of affection, or in a fitting way enjoying the good Creation, or to decline consultation and personal responsibility. Where this, in certain periods, has been interpreted thus (undoubtedly with very sincere intentions), severity which was not aimed at growth and liberation has sometimes initially led to forms of monastic life that appear to thrive in ways that are quantitatively impressive. But not infrequently it caused deep personal wounds as well, it shrank emotional life, did not allow talents to flourish sufficiently (giving someone orders which did not fit his talents was supposed to be "good" for humility), and led here and there to a deep crisis in monastic life. Such a crisis can only be overcome by practical contact with the original Benedictine intentions and to express these in a flexible and dignified manner in the context of our time.

In the area of the so-called "resourcing," an extraordinary amount of work has been done in the monastic world during the past decades, which, however, in many cases still waits to be tackled in earnest.

However, in a sense the "derived" vows of chastity, poverty, and obedience (provided they are properly understood) may be given a place in other forms of living and working together. A family situation does not usually flourish when parents keep changing their ways of cultivating intimate contact, when parents and children constantly quibble about things (even if it is only about shutting off the TV), when parents are inconsistent in their decision-making and/or they are cleverly outsmarted or played against each other.

Neither does a school or business prosper when cliques and other "groups" concentrate on their own interests only, when people individually or as a group lay claim on the "resources" of the institution (while quietly making a maximum personal profit on it), when decisions are quietly or openly sabotaged and derailed.

The positive complement of this is that families, institutions, and businesses prosper with a steady commitment to the whole, a manner of dealing with things and goods that promotes a common commitment, a situation in which, in their very different ways, all noses point in the same direction, because their goals are identical: an affectively bound group of people who are important to each other, a living school that wishes to promote growth, a financial and socially profitable company in which people have a heart for business and for one another.

Thus, in such types of community, appropriate forms of chastity, poverty, and obedience may well be used. Just as, conversely, wrong forms of chastity, poverty, and obedience can work out just as disastrously as in monastic life: when I impulsively recoil from any form of affection for another woman than my spouse, when a school administration at the conclusion of a difficult merger, out of misplaced frugality, does not dare to organize a festive, fraternizing dinner with new colleagues, when a manager in a true reign of terror wrings the neck of any sort of creativity in his organization.

Still stronger than the just-named "derived" vows are the fruitful translation of the original Benedictine vows of *stabilitas*, *conversatio morum*, and *obedientia* into forms of living and working together outside of the monastery.

STABILITAS: Sticking with It, not Walking Away

The vow of *stabilitas* deals with a maintained and steady commitment of action. After a long process of preparation and working together, the monk or nun has freely decided to give a complete "yes" to life according to the rule, under an abbot, and in a certain community. This community then needs to be taken seriously. Because such a monastic community was mostly founded in a certain place and could for the most part provide for its own needs, the term *stabilitas loci* is used: permanence of place. However, that did *not* originally mean that one could never "get out." There was nothing wrong with leaving the monastery for a time when that was necessary for the interest of the community or for the individual monk. The important thing was to be and to remain committed to the community and the abbey that one had chosen. Benedict understood well that this is an essential condition for a fruitful and salutary community life. It would not be helpful if monks, who are constantly on the move, would stop by now and then, if people with a limited commitment wish to keep their options open, so that they might walk away at will if they should dislike something or are disappointed. *Stabilitas* is therefore in the first place, and most obviously: to remain with your community and not walk away from the context you have chosen.

But there is, of course, far more to it than steadiness of place and faithfully remaining with the group. This is not about remaining steady though you are gritting your teeth because you have obligated yourself contractually or some other way, but rather because of the steadiness of the commitment you have given *from your heart*. From the heart, that needs to be maintained, patiently, also with disappointments and pain—which are unavoidable in any form of working or living together. I once heard from an experienced monk who claimed that he, after a period of warm enthusiasm and spiritual growth, did not feel anything in his personal prayer and during the liturgy in chapel for a period of more than ten years. No clear causes were indicated for this situation, such as a worsening atmosphere among the brothers or a bad spiritual example of the abbot or other leaders. It was a period of great spiritual barrenness for him. "Then I learned the meaning of *stabilitas:* carrying on patiently and full of faith. And one day, God knows why, it began to flow again." *Stabilitas* is carrying on, even when this renewed flow is not guaranteed at all, even when it appears as if things will *never* go right again.

Another word for the durability of which Benedict spoke is *faithfulness*. It is not static either—a vow once spoken and a fixed promise—but a movable virtue: a lifelong road in which your identity moves along with the preparedness to stay with the other, and the others, even if they change (less beautiful, duller than before, getting sick, becoming difficult, etc.). Faithfulness can be very difficult, but it can sometimes unexpectedly give a new impulse to your work or relationship. In difficult situations a special talent for listening is needed that can sensitively catch what is possible, where chances exist, how one may handle a situation creatively. It is a natural inclination to concentrate on what is wrong, what cannot be done, where the other person will not budge, a fixation which easily leads to some form of "walking away," whether outwardly or inwardly. For it is, of course, quite possible to maintain outward *stabilitas*, but to walk away inwardly, to actually be absent, though you may remain among your brothers and sisters.

There are many circumstances which may drive away your attention, your commitment, and your dedication, even without it being noticed in a more formal and outward sense. It is possible to share table and bed with someone while maintaining a great distance. The durability of the "yes word" which you once gave is gone—but even if a distance is very great, it can always be diminished somewhat by a little word or a small gesture.

You may arrive on time as teacher in your class, having prepared your lesson, having checked the papers, maintaining reasonably good discipline, while your heart is no longer in it and the spirit is gone. You don't study your subject anymore; neither do you widen your horizon in other ways. And those who no longer cultivate intellectual excitement cannot inspire it in others; it is a negative spiral. What might help to get beyond this is in some ways obvious: start studying in your subject again and widen your horizon by orienting yourself on worthwhile sources. For example, you might reserve a half-hour every day for absorbing yourself in your profession and free a quarter of an hour for something where you might pay close attention to something enjoyable: poetry, music (not background music of course), a spiritual text—as long as it is *worthwhile*, something of value. This habit should be kept up for a few years. Your students will notice your renewed commitment.

Like this teacher, monks have fixed periods in their daily schedule for study and spiritual (= widening of horizon) reading. That this must happen daily shows that the *stabilitas* or endurance is not a static but a dynamic virtue. Every day offers countless possibilities for walking away, but offers just as many opportunities for commitment. Also, when conceived as *stabilitas loci*, this virtue can be translated into nonmonastic situations: the important thing is to bloom where you are planted, in your situation, in your family, in your organization, where you have given your "yes" *and not somewhere else.*

How much escapist daydreaming we spend on thoughts such as: if only it were next week, I wish that this thing was ready, I wish I worked someplace else, if only the children had left, if only I had another partner, if only I could start all over. . . . Not only are such daydreams unrealistic (since they conflict with the situation here and now) but they draw away attention and energy, so that what the present situation demands of us receives insufficient response. Literally, that makes us *irresponsibly* busy.

But we can practice controlling the entry of daydreams bit by bit—and who does not have them?—and at the same time turn our attention around as it were and direct it to what occupies us, or to whoever demands our attention. Practicing alertness will gradually bear fruit. If you sit in a class that seems dull, though you would have preferred to stay in your comfortable bed, you may participate attentively. If it is done attentively, it automatically becomes less dull, and when your involvement and gradually nurtured interest prompts a relevant question, that might stimulate the teacher and your fellow students to heighten their own alertness and attention.

In every context we might practice alertness in one way or another, in the faithfulness the moment demands of us: in a telephone conversation, in your work as maintenance mechanic of a Boeing 747 of El Al, in the preparation of a meal for your family, in your participation in a meeting of the group council, in your contact with a colleague during a reception, while repairing a leaking bicycle tire. In all of these things the rule applies: things prosper when we pay attention to them—and we ourselves prosper at the same time. Naturally, this basic and unspectacular method will often fail to produce miracles, but at least a small improvement of quality is bound to result.

CONVERSATIO MORUM:
DAILY IMPROVEMENT IN MANAGEMENT

The daily practice of averting daydreaming, but instead, turning to the person expecting a response from us, is an example of the fleshing out of the second Benedictine vow: that of *conversatio* (or *conversio*) *morum*, the changing of habits or lifestyle. The example of the teacher who realizes that his commitment is in deep crisis, who then cultivates the habit of studying a half an hour a day and paying attention to something beautiful for fifteen minutes, illustrates this.

Using contemporary jargon, we might say: this is about "turnaround management," but on a very modest microlevel, namely, of yourself. But if you can also inspire others this way—for it is duly noted when the foreman suddenly listens attentively to the input of his workers on the factory floor, when one of the construction workers leaves his work place neat while others do not, etc.—then this Benedictine approach of "improvement management" on a microlevel will lead to a more blessed result than when everything is going to pieces.

Instead of an unrealizable "everything needs to be done totally differently," the Benedictine vow of the *conversatio morum* relates to what ancient philosophical schools taught about a change of lifestyle: attempting it with small, realizable things. Make a habit of these small improvements. Instead of surfing thirty TV channels for fifteen minutes before bedtime (really a waste of time), you might use those fifteen minutes to listen to beautiful music. You will then put a different head on your pillow. At first, you will need to push yourself to do this, but after a while it becomes automatic. An academician with a busy management function—every fifteen minutes a different job on the board, half of which cannot be solved at the moment, though they demand attention—laments that he has no time for concentrated reading anymore, could get used to getting up a half-hour earlier, spending that time on his studies. No one can take that away from you during the rest of your unpredictably busy day. And keep at it every day. After a year you will be surprised how many books you have attentively read. In everyone's life some things may be found where a daily and continuing "turnaround" (or, to use an old-fashioned word: conversion) may be accomplished.

As with *stabilitas*, *conversatio morum* is about dynamic growth and a lifestyle directed toward positive growth. Certainly, getting rid of bad habits cannot do any harm, but more important is the learning of feasible *good* habits. This is about a modest discipline which needs to be maintained, the discipline of daily listening and responding to what is asked of us, of *obedience*.

OBEDIENTIA: ANSWERING EACH OTHER'S CALL

The word *obedientia* is derived from *ob-audire,* a strengthened form of *audire* (= to hear, to listen). As with *ausculta,* this is about especially good hearing, about listening very attentively, being obedient.

Being *obedient* sounds old-fashioned and calls forth associations with servile situations: executing orders blindly, excluding reason (and certainly the heart), "slave discipline," keeping subordinates small, making yourself as subordinate small, despotism. . . . These associations are not cited gratuitously, because we know enough examples where "obedience" is imaged in one or more of these ways: in the family situation, in class, in church, in the monastery, in business, in a government assembly. Such freedom-curtailing obedience is seldom a *blessing,* and it is certainly not Benedictine. Neither is giving only an outward response—while grumbling inwardly—because an authority orders it, for that is not giving a response from the heart and freely taking responsibility. Such a form of obedience dulls many of our talents toward growth, as Lonergan has mapped out so eloquently.

Obedientia is also a dynamic vow, targeting growth. It is about hearing with the heart. As the eye catches light and the ear sound, so one who listens with the heart tries to catch *meaning* to discover the sensible in a situation. When we say that we take people and things to heart, that is more than registering what we hear or conclude; then, we want to be open to the appeal which a situation or person addresses to us.

When obedience is conceived thus, we might propose that its opposite is not disobedience, but *absurdity,* from *ab-surdus,* to be stone-deaf to something. When we say that something is absurd, we are deaf to its meaning. But with a sensitive, discerning ear we can catch a sensible appeal even in a situation that appears absurd, even in a concentration camp, as we can discover in the works of Primo Levi and Alexander Solzhenitsyn.

Obedience is not the end of personal freedom, but a beginning point of liberation: the cracking of the thick crust around my "I" and the orienting of myself to who or what has something to say to me. That may certainly also entail that I acknowledge authority in the other: the master of a certain trade, the mature person whom I may accompany, an insight offering me an orientation, the expert who knows the ropes, my coworker in the factory who, as manager, brings me in contact with reality. Obedience is therefore also: allowing others to tell you something, being *willing* to listen to advice, and giving up of my conceit as difficult as it may be. Obedience is first of all an internal *positive* response, not outward conforming to prevent punishment and sanctions. To respond often goes together with losing and finding oneself at the same time. We often feel best when we, in a strict sense, "are not ourselves," but are wrapped up in something that interests us, fascinates us or somehow appeals to us. That is when life flourishes, and then we flourish at the same time. To be disobedient in this view is not simply failure to conform to instructions, rules, commands, and commanders. To be disobedient is: giving no response, not being "with it," missing signals, ignoring opportunities—a kind of spiritual error that we rightly indicate as "sin."

(Dis)obedience in the Benedictine sense is easily translated into situations outside of the monastery. When I, at night, review the day to see what happened to my promise of *obedientia*, I do not ask myself first of all whether I have bravely followed the rules given me from higher up, but rather whether I am alert in situations where I am expected to respond. In the meeting I chaired, did I listen to the points others introduced to arrive at a balanced and solid decision, or had I already made up my mind, and was the so-called round of consultation of coworkers nothing but a ritual dance? Did I react sufficiently attentively to my daughter when she let me know that she was concerned about something, or did I quickly, in good humor but superficially, move on to a less threatening subject? Did I take the questions of my students seriously or did I use them only to make my next brilliant point? They are all opportunities for (dis)obedience. I purposely selected examples where I could, seen superficially, have my say. For (dis)obedience is not at all a matter for children alone, for subordinates and those who are placed lower. In fact, the vow of *obedientia* remains valid for the *abbot* also. When important decisions must be made in the monastery, it is *his* turn to listen very carefully to the brothers' comments. In other places of the Rule also, much is demanded of the abbot in terms of good listening to what people and situations demand of him. We do not only obey superiors. The CEO of a multinational corporation, the conductor of an orchestra, or a bishop, may cultivate *obedientia* in this sense. We may put it even stronger: to the extent that they in a certain sense value highly their coworkers, musicians, or diocesans, and respect them as sources of value in a fitting manner, their business, orchestra, or diocese will prosper and flourish. And when a company, orchestra, or diocese does not flourish, there the suspicion arises that the CEO, conductor, or bishop was insufficiently "obedient."

3. *Additional Aspects of the Benedictine Art of Listening*

HOSPITALITY: ANY GUEST MAY BE THE LORD

Hospitality is a special form of obedience (like listening to one another): answering someone's call. At the beginning of chapter 53 on the receiving of guests, the *Rule* says:[4] "Let all guests who arrive be received like Christ, for He is going to say, 'I came as a guest, and you received Me.'" Realizing that any guest may be the Lord, the porter is instructed to answer as soon as someone knocks, or when a poor person asks for help: "Thanks be to God" *(Deo gratias)* or: "Let us bless the Lord" *(Benedicamus Domino).*

Any guest may be the Lord, but the Lord may look very shabby. Sometimes we need to pay close attention and look beyond appearances to see the contours of the Lord in the other person. And as a listening doctor must listen very attentively, distinguishing between all sorts of noise, to catch those signals

[4] All citations from Benedict's *Rule* are from: *St. Benedict's Rule for Monasteries.* Translated by Leonard J. Doyle. Collegeville: The Liturgical Press, 1948.

demanding an adequate response, so we need, in all our conversations with our "guests," to put out our antennas so that we may experience the other person as a source of the Spirit. We need to work hard so that we may be attentive receivers of the Spirit.

That may sound pious and demanding—and that is what it is. Fortunately, attentive hospitality may be improved and cultivated by means of small qualitative impulses. It lends itself splendidly—like everything worthwhile—for the *conversio morum*. Two everyday applications of "Benedictine hospitality" may clarify that, namely, telephone conversations and receptions.

Each telephone conversation is a question of hospitality, of listening, and responding—at least that is what it should be. But when the phone rings our spontaneous reaction is to view it as a disturbance, as an interruption of our work or even more important, as the entry of a trespasser. Though we feel rather irritated, our reaction is often anticipated: "Am I disturbing you? Do you have a minute? You must be busy, is it convenient?" Our irritation and discomfort sometimes have a physical result: when we put the phone down we still see its imprint in our hand. There is another way, however. To accept a telephone conversation as a chance to receive a guest. When the phone rings, wait a moment before you pick it up, perhaps to change your inner attitude a little: from irritation to hospitality. To help myself with this I often say a little mental "prayer of blessing" for my still unknown guest: *Benedicamus Domino*—it might be the Lord! My change of attitude, no matter how modestly it may have succeeded, may well be sensed on the other end of the line. The conversation may well have a somewhat different tone and content.

Receptions are intended to be a hospitable meeting with many opportunities for listening and responding—but those chances are all too often missed. Who does not know the phenomenon conveniently labeled the "reception look"? You are in conversation with someone during a reception, but you notice that his look is out of focus because he is looking at something beside you, in the direction of someone who is more important than you, someone with whom he would really much rather talk. When that new conversation is then begun, the same thing is likely to happen. Quite regularly I observe at receptions the rather absurd situation where *both* partners, engaged in what appears to be a conversation, are looking for other persons who are more interesting. This absurd situation also lends itself well for a small injection of Benedictine quality: by turning the look back a few degrees (*conversio* in a literal sense) and to concentrate on the person with whom you are speaking. The attention then concentrates automatically: when you are looking at someone, you will automatically ask real questions, listen genuinely, become interested, and respond. The conversation will gain in quality—perhaps only a little— and perhaps your own *conversio* will work contagiously. Your conversation partner will notice your attention and interest and possibly concentrate more on the one with whom he is conversing.

It is not difficult to mention and develop many analogous opportunities for listening hospitality: with the conducting of conversations relating to job applications and interviews (those who lead them always need to have a "stethoscope" with them), during meetings (how seldom do people listen carefully to each other), in the contact with new colleagues after an organizational fusion, with the welcoming of your new director or bishop (again, take a stethoscope along!).

DECISION-MAKING CONSULTATION

A meeting is indeed a good opportunity for cultivating the art of listening. The practice is of course different: meetings are held in the most varying organizations in which people hardly listen to one another. We only need to check our own experience: how seldom does it happen that one of the participants in a meeting enters the gathering with a certain viewpoint, and explains and defends that viewpoint, but after listening carefully to the comments of others, informs the others that he is revising his viewpoint because the proposal made by someone else is better than his own? Such a change (another form of *conversio*) should really be very normal—a gathering should also serve to come to the *best* solution which is not necessarily *mine*—but many would consider that as "getting a slap," as a defeat.

Our customary attitude in a gathering may be very different. We wait until *our* point of view gets a turn and then we want to score. Or we watch how we can pull unexpectedly the legs from under the chair of our opponents. Or we slyly search for procedural opportunities to get our way. A gathering is often more of an arena than a thoughtful deliberation of people sharing a concern—even if we may keep up appearances: "But didn't we agree that . . . "; "all noses must point the same way"; "but according to our mission statement . . . "

Abbeys are also the scene where regular decision-making or deliberations preparatory to decision-making take place. Benedict offers a few suggestions for the way in which this should happen; they are very broadly useful:

> Whenever any important business has to be done in the monastery, let the Abbot call together the whole community and state the matter to be acted upon. Then, having heard the brethren's advice, let him turn the matter over in his own mind and do what they shall judge to be most expedient. The reason we have said that all should be called for counsel is that the Lord often reveals to the younger what is best.
>
> (Quoted from chapter 3: On Calling the Brethren for Counsel.)

We can well imagine that many a novice (aspiring monk or sister) would underline this last sentence in his or her copy of the *Rule*.

When we read this text attentively, several elements are noticed. "Whenever any *important business* has to be done in the monastery, let the *Abbot* call together *the whole community*." In other words: less important matters the abbot himself can decide, whether or not assisted by a few members of his management team (prior, economist, or novice master). But if something is more important, the more the well-being of the entire community is involved, the greater the circle needs to be which the abbot consults. This is very different from what often happens in business and for that matter, elsewhere where the circle of decision-making becomes smaller the more important the question is: with an organizational fusion, dealings with the Stock Exchange, with an extensive reorganization, often only the management team or only the management council or ultimately only the chairman and his partner are involved in conversation or negotiation. There may be valid reasons for such a procedure, but a strong argument may be made for Benedict's approach. Precisely by enlarging the circle of consultation, the commitment of those who must eventually bear and execute an important decision is enlarged simultaneously. That commitment will be greater to the extent that one knows from experience that such a consultation is taken seriously—that the abbot also really *listens*. In leadership an extra talent for listening is needed, as well as the capacity to distinguish between matters that may be decided in a small circle and matters where a broader consultation is appropriate.

"[A]nd state the matter to be acted upon." How great is the temptation *not* to do that! It is easy for the one ultimately responsible to assign the job of stating the agenda to one of lower rank. That has two advantages: when the proposal does not work out well, someone else is put down; moreover, it saved him the trouble to consider the matter well ahead of time. Another tactic is to sketch only a few vague contours and then hope that sufficient useful material pops up in the exchange to incorporate into a proposal a majority may accept. Benedict has a different view. The abbot must enter the consultation well prepared, after moreover having considered whether the issue is important enough to consult the *entire* community. Then, he himself needs to say what the issue is: What is the question? What is important in this? On what conditions does a solution need to be sought? What type of solutions does the abbot envisage? "Then, having heard the brethren's advice . . ." Now it is up to the abbot to *listen: audiens consilium. . . .* It is not easy, after the exposition of your own standpoint, to really open your ears and catch the explicit and implicit signals which might impinge on your decision-making. It is very tempting for the leader to let everyone have their say, without really taking other opinions seriously and then to "decide" that such opinions are only nursed along for the form; after all, you had already decided what you wanted before the consultation!

The abbot must listen just as seriously as the student in the first sentence of the *Rule:* it should make him think. "Let him turn the matter over in his own mind . . ." The Latin text *tractet apud se* makes it even clearer that this is not just a distant "cognitive" considering, but that the abbot himself must be involved in this, and from the heart.

"[A]nd do *[fecit]* what he shall judge to be most expedient." Here we see the return of the triad of the first sentence of the Rule. There it was: listen attentively, agree heartily, and execute in deed. Here it is: listening to counsel, considering, and deciding to act. That is to say, action which is the most "useful," that means: action which contributes most to the growth and flourishing of the community. An interesting further qualification is given to the listening to *everyone's* counsel: "The Lord often reveals to the younger what is best." Indeed, it is always worthwhile to listen attentively to the advice of those who are new and fresh in your organization, who have not yet been affected too much by the beaten path and internal *mores*. "Young" is surely not only to be judged by age. Sometimes there are old-timers who have kept themselves fresh by regularly working on widening their horizons.

The decision-making sketched above is not democratic. After a careful process of consultation the leader must himself take and bear responsibility for his decisions. He cannot hide behind a majority of voices or behind the excuse of not knowing alternate possibilities, for they surely would have come up during a careful consultation process. This is management responsibility in *optima forma: you* need to give the right response to what the situation and the organization ask of you—and only then you are also approachable.

No Grumbling

When there is bad listening in a consultation process, either by a monk or by an abbot, a climate of grumbling is often the result. Listening has its complement in grumbling. Just as obedience is a positive attitude, wanting to listen before anyone has spoken, grumbling is a kind of negative speech before attentive listening, or also because listening has not been done attentively.

Benedict regards grumbling as a serious sin; not less than twelve times *murmuratio* is named in the *Rule* as a serious threat to the community. In an organization, grumbling works as a slowly and subconsciously working social poison. Grumbling obscures vision, drains energy, and touches the heart. This is true for "internal" as well as "external" grumbling. Those who internally grumble and complain can no longer see clearly and listen—because another voice is already speaking, their attention and energy is directed to something other than what is going on at the moment, and therefore they cannot do their task any longer "from the heart." External grumbling is even more damaging, because it spreads like an unregulated division of cells; we call it griping [Dutch: *kankeren*] for good reason. Grumblers seek each other's company, strengthen one another and infect others; they act like sand and poison in your organization. Griping has its own way of spreading: doing poor work, stalling, letting others wait—these are the weapons with which subordinates indirectly attack their bosses. We shall return to this subject in the following chapter on Benedictine leadership.

Fortunately, there is an antidote against grumbling, namely, *cheerfulness*. The term may sound rather old-fashioned and naïve. Dictionaries define this word as being of a cheerful spirit, or good-humored (as opposed to dejected), accepting even sorrow and adversity. This last meaning says that this is not about cranked up optimism, blind to what is wrong and difficult. Cheerfulness has to do with being courageous—a character trait not needed when everything works smoothly, but only when we meet barriers, adversity, worry, and uncertainty.

Benedictine cheerfulness—as antidote against *murmuratio*—is a wise alliance of attentive listening (without closing one's ears to what sounds less pleasant), of consultations (also by the weak, elderly, the "crippled," the marginal persons, the quiet ones, and especially the grumblers), of dignified good humor, of an upbeat word, particularly in difficult circumstances. Such cheerfulness is a slowly working social balm, an elixir that gives renewed strength.

This is not something "soft," which spirituality should not be (if it is, that is a signal for its wanting quality). Spirituality is about *élan vital*, life orientation, and organization of life,[5] and that is exactly what cheerfulness aims at: modeling, even in difficult situations, an infectious and exemplary *élan* and offering an orientation which sees a situation with different eyes. That enables us to stand up unexpectedly against something overpowering, when an impossible chore appears manageable, looking like a labyrinth but with an exit, appearing that you have more bounce in you than you had thought.

We all know examples of this type of situation and of people who inspire us to transcend ourselves: the director who gets his people to play music literally at the edge of their chair; the manager who, with a smile and a good example, gets his coworkers to finish tasks which, with a bully, they would not even have started, or at the most, do half-way; the teacher who makes a class of adolescents forget that this is a "lesson" and gets them to work with passion on a real problem. One might ask: what is their secret—with the secret longing in the back of our mind to solve this riddle and to profit by imitating their success. But in this also the rule applies that imitation is not the genuine product. Your coworkers quickly realize whether that *smile* of yours is rooted in real cheerfulness or only something you picked up at a seminar on management tools. Real fruit always grows quietly as it ripens. Yet it may be instructive to consider what keeps that inspiring conductor, that cheerful manager and that masterful teacher fresh and motivating. How did they get their own *élan*? Where did they acquire their life orientation? How does this express itself in their conduct of life and their lifestyle?

When you ask these people themselves—and I have been able to do so at different times under favorable circumstances—you will get a variety of answers. But these answers have something in common: in the most varying ways they cultivate the conditions of their own *growth*. Just as in nature, growth cannot be forced, though one might cultivate the conditions (or neglect them!) promoting growth.

The conductor constantly engrosses himself in the cultural roots of a musical piece he begins to work on: he reads novels,

[5] This beautiful description is by Theo Zweerman and Jozef Wissink.

poetry, philosophy, history. That is how he widens his horizon beyond that of the score and the musical profession alone. Managers of large organizations whom I asked about their "spirituality" told about their own ways to keep their spirits fresh. One reads something pleasant or inspiring before retiring—no matter how late—for always exactly an hour. Someone else rises an hour earlier than necessary and takes a walk on the beach, no matter what the weather. The executive chairman of a large company listed on the Stock Exchange keeps bees (he is a certified beekeeper) and sheep—an activity that requires daily effort and attention. The teacher cultivates her own profession (a rarity among teachers): she studies, publishes, and takes graduate courses in foreign universities. And she paints icons. What common elements may be observed? They all work to widen horizons, they seek situations where silence and reflection can flourish, they make contact with sources of value—not incidentally, but regularly. Benedict would nod in agreement. This is precisely what he had in mind with the *daily* spiritual reading with which he charges his monks, the *lectio divina*.

THE LECTIO DIVINA:
KEEPING IN CONTACT WITH SOURCES OF VALUE

Lectio divina is the exact opposite of the diagonal *scanning* of text with a green marker, to quickly highlight the keywords and main points that might be important for a negotiation session or for a meeting. After that you may forget them again. The spiritual reading Benedict prescribes for his monks was intended in the old monasteries, among other things, to be learned *by heart*. The *lectio divina* is about a *very slow reading* of a text, preferably aloud, that the words may really be mouthed and tasted. This is reading till a word or phrase *touches* you, till you listen to something that as it were sticks to you. This word or phrase is then repeated aloud, regurgitated, as it were. The Latin term for this process is *ruminatio*—simply what you see cows doing in a quiet place, preparing the product of the first digestive process for the following phase in the transformation of grass into milk. During intervening moments this word or phrase is unpacked: what does it say to me? What touches me in this reading? Why does it touch *me*? What might it mean *within my context*? How might I fruitfully *respond* to it? This is about as it were to tap the text from all sides and to listen to it with the stethoscope—not because of voluntary interest, but so that I might give an adequate response to it. With the *ruminatio* we try to press a maximum of nutritional juices out of a piece of text. Then we keep reading slowly, till we suspect we have landed again on something nutritional.

This transformation process has a *double* significance: the text is transformed—because it is brought over and "translated" into my context; and I, the reader, am changed. Sometimes only a little: I need to look at this question differently. Sometimes a text can open up so unexpectedly that an inward vista shows itself in which you as it were keep "hanging" for a while. Monastic literature mentions the four phases or steps of the *lectio divina:* the *lectio,* the *meditatio,* the *oratio* (prayer), and the *contemplatio.* Translated: do a slow reading till you are tripped, with repetition and association, responding, open-mouthed, gratefully looking into the depth or into the distance.

These four phases of increasing deepening are, of course, not always experienced by any means. Often we experience just staying the course in *lectio* and *meditatio.* Those are also the only phases we can *work* on. Whether a word or phrase speaks to you in a manner that a hearty response may be given remains to be seen (a monk once defined his prayer meditation as "sitting and waiting"). One cannot organize unexpected vistas. Moreover, a text may contain some thistles. A text may be nicely locked up, but the reader may as well. "That text says nothing to me (yet)," will often be the reaction. Benedict would say: "Did you listen attentively enough? Did you use your stethoscope? Did you *only* hear noise?"

A Church Father like Augustine of Hippo must have been a master in the *lectio divina.* When one reads his commentaries on the Psalms, vista after vista opens up. A contemporary equal is the Dutch poet Gerrit Komrij who can masterfully illuminate line after line of a poem to such an extent that the text really *opens up* for you.[6] How much quiet, persistent, and attentive reading must have preceded this!

The persistent attitude of reading and meditation with the *lectio divina* reminds us of the triad of the first sentence of the *Rule:* listen attentively, agree heartily, give a realistic response. One can also recognize the three vows in it: *stabilitas,* quietly persisting; *conversio morum,* transformation; and *obedientia,* listening.

Such daily sustained contact with sources of value can also be fruitful and inspiring outside of the monastery walls. The sources of value can vary greatly: texts, illustrations, music, nature. . . . One can draw *life élan* from it, meet life orientations, be called to a different manner of organizing life. Cultivating this contact offers the extension of horizon and creates the preconditions for growth and development. This insight is very strikingly expressed in *Psalm 1,* which lends itself (as do all the psalms) very well for the *lectio divina.* Here follows a translation of this psalm[7] which follows the original Hebrew text very closely and is inspired by the German rendering of Martin Buber:[8]

> O the happiness of the man
> who does not walk in the counsel of the wicked,
> and in the way of sinners does not stand,
> and in the seat of scoffers does not sit.
> But in the Torah of the LORD is his delight.
> And in his Torah he meditates by day and by night.
> He is like a tree
> planted by streams of water,
> which gives its fruit in its time,
> and its leaves do not wilt.
> And everything he does, succeeds.

[6] Cf. Gerrit Komrij, *In Liefde Bloeyende* (Amsterdam, 1998).

[7] Private translation by Martin Kessler.

[8] The unique translation by Rosenzweig and Buber was only completed in the 1960s. The current edition of the volume in which the Psalms occur is: *Die Schrift verdeutscht von Martin Buber gemeinsam mit Franz Rosenzweig, 4. Das Buch der Preisungen.* Stuttgart: Deutsche Bibelgesellschaft, 1992.

> Not so are the wicked,
> but they are like chaff which the wind blows away.
> Therefore the wicked will not stand in the judgment,
> nor sinners in the congregation of the righteous,
> For the LORD knows the way of the righteous,
> But the way of the wicked will be lost.

This psalm might be titled: "The Man Who Has Chosen." The word "has" should be nuanced, however, for this is not about a once-for-all, single choice; we are daily challenged to make choices. Each choice made may either be fruitful or run dead (be lost). What steps do I take? What influences my orientation? The metaphors "walking" and the choosing of the right "way" color this psalm: "the man who does not *walk* in the counsel of the wicked," and "in the *way* of the evildoers does not *stand*," "the Lord knows the *way* of the righteous," "the *path* of the wicked will be lost."

People familiar with the desert know how vitally important is a correct orientation: the right route leads to somewhere, the wrong takes you nowhere, it loses itself, it breaks off. The same is true for one's life orientation: there are valuable sources of orientation, and there are worthless directions. What matters is to be sufficiently open to make contact with sources of value, to distinguish them from what is worthless, and ever to choose a way that bears fruit. In this respect I am not primarily thinking of dramatic life decisions; some decisions are, of course, dramatic: one may make the radical decision to quit a worthless lifestyle, or one may adopt a lifestyle where one may grow and flourish. I am also thinking of the many little choices made daily, any one of which can "inject" value or nonvalue, balm or poison into the causal network of my life. Listening attentively to a coworker or hinting that you have something more important to do, writing that letter to someone experiencing difficulties, or preferring to spend time on that interesting article in a journal, reading to your children before they go to bed, or a quick goodnight kiss because you are still so busy, with a friendly gesture adding someone to the agenda, a quarter of an hour of Bach before going to bed, or carelessly surfing worthless TV programs, paying attention in a staff conversation about the strong points and the possibilities for growth of a coworker, or delivering cynical commentary to where he went wrong. It is striking that in this text the sources of nonvalue are always *people:* the wicked, the sinner, the scoffer, who call up and strengthen resentment—the violators of what is valuable, the brazen—bold figures without embarrassment, the sinners, who commit sin against time, the sin of choosing to mix with them, the cynics and the grumblers. They seek each others' company; they are "the counsel of the wicked," "the circle of the mockers." It is very tempting to contribute your own worthless pebble, or start your own little circle of grumblers and mockers.

And the sources of value? They, too, are persons and ultimately related to a person. How must we choose? "The Torah (law) of the Lord."[9] That may not sound very appealing at first. But this is not about "law" in a juridical sense, like a code of justice. Buber's translation of *Torah [Weisung]* suggests that it is rather a "direction pointer" than a collection of juridical rules, the transgression of which is punished by sanctions. It is a law in whose teaching you take delight, it gives joy, for the law offers points of orientation by which you may prosper. That *Weisung*[10] is always handed on to us by others: texts, such as this psalm, music, exemplary figures, teachers, your children. It is good to reflect on what they are handing on to you, and not too hastily pass it by: "on his Torah he meditates by day and by night." "Meditating" sounds rather intellectual; in Buber the words of value are related to the mouth: "about his teaching *(Weisung)* he mumbles *[murmelt]* day and night."

Choosing what is valuable is not so much a question of sticking bravely to the rules. This text teaches us that this is about *fruitfulness,* which results when your roots reach out to where "water is streaming." That may be a daily question: was I rooted today in streaming, living water? Am I looking for that? When

---

[9] The Torah in the first place refers to the Pentateuch and by extension to the Old Testament.

[10] This is Buber's title for the Pentateuch. The name is derived from the verb meaning "to point."

I note signals of withering in myself and others, do I then reach for streaming water, for myself and for them?

That is indeed a necessary condition for fruitfulness, but certainly not a guarantee for immediate growth and flourishing: "who bears fruit *in season*," or, more emphatically as Buber translates, "which *in its time* gives *its* fruit." Often much patience is needed; "in *its* time" may be quite distant; moreover, we need to respect that this is about "*its* fruit." One of the monks of the abbey to which I am related has busied himself for more than five decades with miniatures and texts of Hildegard of Bingen. That gradually produced some fruit and insights, but only shortly after his eightieth year came something that was also fruitful for others. Moreover, it was "*his* fruit," not a contribution to science, but the associative and horizon-widening perspective of the artist. Even at an advanced age, this foliage was not at all withered. With the verse "which in *its time* gives *its* fruit," I often think of this monk, Henri Boelaars— but I also mumble it quietly when a colleague or dear friend has not yet produced the fruits which you had so much hoped for. Sometimes I myself need to leave a project alone for a little while or sometimes longer, because of other priorities. In that case it may be a "de-stressing" and "slowing down" rule of life: "who in *its time* gives *its* fruit."

Rooted where water streams, one bears fruit in season and grows. But what if one does not maintain contact with sources of value? Then, no growth is visible, then you are like chaff that the wind blows away. Not so much as "punishment" from on high, but because what is coming out of you is not rooted, does not persist; it has no power to live. This is an experience I will share with many: some of your projects resemble loose sand, they are insufficiently anchored, they are lifeless. Entire processes can run through your fingers and arrive on a dead track.

The final verse of Psalm 1 shows that this is not about *external* reward or punishment, but about *intrinsic* fruitfulness or the lack of it. No avenging angel with a flaming sword stands at the end of the path of the wicked; this path comes out in loose sand, it breaks off: "the way of the evildoer loses itself." That is how one gets lost.

And the way of those who "go the right way," the way of the "kept ones" who orient themselves on sources of value? There is no reward at the end for them either. Fruitfulness appears on the way. We read only that the Lord *knows* his way or, what is synonymous in Hebrew, that the Lord *loves* this way. It is not prescribed, no reward is promised nor punishment threatened. We need to choose ourselves, and do so constantly, orienting ourselves on the sources of value others hand to us. It is your *own* way which bears fruit or only makes some chaff whirl up. And if we are honest, we are always both *kept ones* and *evil-doers*, both fruitful and barren. Fortunately, each day offers opportunities for *conversio morum*, for small changes of direction. Not out of courage or driven by conformity, but because we thrive better through this. That is said at the outset in the first words of this psalm: "O the happiness of the man" is not a descriptive "indicative," as if to say: look at the man who has made the happy choice. It is rather an exclamation: "O the *happiness* of the man . . ." With a right choice, joy increases simultaneously. The choice for ongoing contact with sources of value, for example in the manner of the *lectio divina*, is a beautiful example of this.

PART III

Benedictine Leadership: Stimulating People toward Growth[1]

1. *Leadership Demands a Special Talent for Listening*

At a getting acquainted period at the opening of a weekend of reflection with a number of entrepreneurs, I asked whether they had brought something tangible that might symbolize "good leadership" to them. There were divergent and interesting reactions. They nodded with approval at the image of a baton used in races: one enters a situation that already exists and thus inherits what has been done in the past toward creating a business culture. In time, you will take a turn at passing on the baton, on which you have naturally left your fingerprints and stamp, whether they be beautiful or ugly. Someone else had taken along a can of copper polish: an organization which appears to shine also needs daily care, sometimes quite basic, to keep it shining.

I would have brought a *stethoscope* as a symbol of Benedictine leadership. The art of listening stands primary in Benedictine life. Those who bear extra responsibility in the community need to possess special talents relative to attentive listening and responding adequately. The chapters in the *Rule* about the abbot and the economist *(cellarius)* of the monastery offer

[1] The author gratefully acknowledges his use of the bibliography printed at the end of the text for the material in this chapter.

many small but fundamental pieces of advice for anyone who is responsible for the "care of souls" in one way or another: teachers, parents, bishops, and managers of whatever kind.

Giving leadership is ultimately a question of *spiritual* life. One leads processes, streams of production, organizational networks, the transfer of knowledge, the flow of information, formation of networking, research and development, and whatever terms are presently used in the jargon of management. It is indeed very tempting to the leader not to go deeper and concentrate only on the external and organizational, while avoiding real listening, real conversation and real responding. We easily surrender to this temptation because the external and organizational is easier to handle than the internal and spiritual—including the spirit of the leader himself.

It is like an inattentive physician who discovers a mild case of grippe in a patient that later turns out to be real pneumonia which can only be treated with painkillers and antifever medication. The good doctor uses his stethoscope. It is quite an art to carefully distinguish whether this is bronchitis or an inflammation in the midst of the noise, the beating and the beeping, and then to consider the best course of action.

Good leadership is about something similar. When something is going on in an organization, it is necessary to be alert to catch the first signals. Apply the stethoscope and amidst the noise try to notice, what is going on—however, also when things are going well it is good to listen attentively and to remain in conversation to know what is taking place. To make the correct diagnosis is a question of experience, prudence, intuition, and *sapientia* (the art of "tasting"). Sometimes things work out by themselves, when people are given room and time to straighten them out. Sometimes gentle and sensible adjusting is needed. At other times a surgical invasion may be needed, exact and relevant, with minimum damage and blood loss and solely directed to the good of the organism as a whole—the ultimate goal of the physician.

Leadership is about diagnostic ability, with a vision of the whole, and with the ability to appeal to others in such a way that they begin to move, literally, become *motivated*. This "leading of souls" places demands on one's own soul. The chapters about the abbot and the cellarer in Benedict's *Rule* are not only, or above all, about their tasks and qualifications, but also and above all about the qualities and possibilities for growth of their *own* souls. How should someone be constituted and keep oneself functioning spiritually (for the abbot also needs to think of the "care of his own soul") to provide leadership at all? In theories about good management, questions are often asked about *what* that is, *how* that needs to be done and *why*. Benedict would say that a much more important question precedes this: *who* is giving leadership?

2. *The Person of the Abbot*

The second chapter of the *Rule* highlights which qualities the abbot needs to possess. The following chapter is about the manner of the leaders' decision-making in the monastery (which was discussed above). Chapter 64 deals formally about the appointment of the abbot but also contains a number of supplemental character traits which Benedict hopes to find in a good abbot—even if it sounds rather static: after all, one is able to *grow* in one's leadership function.

Based on fragments from the chapters about the abbot, I wish to examine which anthropological conditions relate to good leadership in Benedict's vision. There is a constant consideration as to what extent different things might be relevant for giving leadership in other contexts than those of an abbey.

> An Abbot who is worthy to be over a monastery should always remember what he is called, and live up to the name of Superior (2.1, p. 7).

> The Abbot should always remember what he is and what he is called, and should know that to whom more is committed, from him more is required. Let him understand also what a difficult and arduous task he has undertaken: ruling souls and adapting himself to a variety of characters. One he must coax, another scold, another persuade, according to each one's character and understanding. Thus he must adjust and adapt himself to all in such a way that he may not only suffer no loss in the flock committed to his care, but may even rejoice in the increase of a good flock (2.30-33, p. 11).

The abbot must "always remember *what he is called*." He is called *abbas*, father. We saw this fatherly aspect already in the opening sentence of the *Rule*, which even speaks of a "loving" father, which is really a pleonasm. A *loveless* father is really not worthy of the name "father."

First off, it probably sounds woolly and soft to expect a form of "loving parent" in a leader outside of the monastic community. But love is not something soft and rosy but a form of commitment given unconditionally from the heart that needs to be cultivated "in good and bad days." In the previous chapter we discussed the five domains which Bernard Lonergan, entirely in the spirit of Benedict, distinguishes in the area of human spiritual growth: the domain of attention, of intelligence, of reasonableness, of responsibility, of the commitment of the heart. These are not steps to be climbed, one after the other, but rather presupposing one another, mutually affecting aspects of a single attitude. Imagine, by way of thinking, a manager, director, or bishop, who in his leadership has achieved a high level of attention, intelligence, reasonableness, and responsibility, but who does not really feel himself committed to his organization, orchestra, or diocese, who does not perform his task from the heart. This will not appear very fruitful in the long run. Quite possibly, on an external level, some progress may have been made: a more structured and effective consultation, more transparent decision-making, better limit-setting of responsibility, a more thorough study of the score and a more homogeneous sound of the orchestra, higher quality of proclamation and liturgy. But on the internal level, ongoing growth will be unlikely: people have their antennas out, sensing when a commitment is not from the heart, just as they "go through the fire" for the one who has "it." Souls can only be put into motion by souls who are moved themselves.

This was indeed about a thought experiment, for on an internal and spiritual level, growth in attention, intelligence, reasonableness, and responsibility is not at all *possible* without concomitant, preceding growth of commitment, given from the heart and cultivated.

From this vantage point, the term "parenthood" is not out of order if we associate it with people who bear extra responsibility in an organization. Parenthood is by definition a commitment which is from the heart and unconditional. A father and mother who take seriously their raising of children in terms of time, care, and attention, but at the same time experience it as an unpleasant duty, can hardly be labeled good parents. Their children will not truly flourish in such a climate, even if they should lack nothing—except what is most essential. Moreover, parenthood is directed toward growth, particularly spiritual growth—the kind of growth that occurs naturally and is not forced, with periods of stagnation in between, with side-shoots and room for "failing"—periods in which affection is not suspended or withdrawn. This pertains to leadership in other contexts as well.

As an example I am thinking of a leader of a scientific research group. Evidently, he needs to stimulate his coworkers toward intellectual growth, if final research results are to be realized. But it is part of the natural course of events that periods of stagnation and aridity will occur, as well as being on the wrong track, which may demand a great deal of exertion, but which apparently lead nowhere, so that the investigators need to retrace their steps. But that need not be a problem: on the way, "wood has been cut," and the realization that something was *not* found (the *docta ignorantia*) or was totally wrong, is intellectually a big (sometimes a very big) jump ahead. An investigator who forbids side-alleys and punishes apparent "failing" with his eye strictly pealed to the result to be achieved will neither be loved nor successful. The great physicist and pedagogue Niels Bohr was a good example of how it should be done. He gave space in an atmosphere of "serious play" (as Hendrik Casimir, one of his very successful young coworkers, characterizes this climate), sent them sometimes intentionally on wrong tracks (from which they sometimes returned with surprises for him), and when things did not work out (and more often when everything went well), he closed his institute for theoretical physics for a few hours and went to see a Western or went swimming with his entire team. This turned out to be an approach which led to so much growth that it has been called "the golden years of physics." Niels Bohr was indeed more of an abbot than a commander. His approach may have been a thorn in the flesh to many contemporaries on the university staff.

All of this does not exclude moments of correction, but it needs to be a correction directed toward the good (well-being) and not toward punishment and revenge—exactly what Benedict expects of the correction by the abbot. We shall return to this aspect of correction.

> Let him understand also what a difficult and arduous task he has undertaken: ruling souls and adapting himself to a variety of characters.

The heart—the heavy and difficult heart—of good leadership is the ruling or leading of souls: to motivate souls, to offer them an orientation, and setting them in an oriented movement. Weak leadership yields to the temptation to ignore this difficult and heavy task and to concentrate on what is easier: everything in which the *human* factor is not primary—structures, financial aspects, the mission statement, the "package."

Why is the "ruling of souls" so difficult? Benedict relates this to "*adapting* himself to a variety of characters." To begin with, such adaptation is difficult. Without reflecting, we tend to associate leadership with the ability to have many services performed, like a king with many servants. But Benedict relates such helpfulness in the first place with those who lead: this one serves *ministrans*, to be serving. And to what object is such service directed? "To a variety of characters." The variety pertains to their own personalities that will be quite diverse. This issues into quite diverging forms of response that Benedict expects from the abbot: "One he must coax, another scold, another persuade." This is difficult indeed: the one leading must both be able to listen carefully to how things are with the souls of the "brothers" and give the right response to each of these brothers. That demands much, but far more from the one who leads than from the one who is led. Again, without reflecting, we find it obvious that the subservient needs to yield and adapt to the wishes and whims of the leader—which indeed happens quite often in practice. Benedict turns the relationships around: the abbot must rule souls by "adapting himself to a variety of characters." Greater responsibility demands greater flexibility. One might comment in this connection that the saying "like monks, like cowls" is valid only for the cowls and other externals. Because the monks are all different internally, the abbot will, carefully listening to everyone, arrive at "unlike" responses. In the area of cowls, unlikeness is not fitting. But in the area of souls, only "unlike" responses are fitting and adequate. Brotherliness does not imply egalitarianism. Differences, when they are good, are not only respected but should even be *cultivated* by a wise abbot.

That is indeed difficult and hard. But such a response, adapted to everyone, is needed, Benedict claims, for the prospering of the community as a whole. The flexibility of the abbot, supported by careful listening and responding, is directed toward the goal "that he may not only suffer no loss in the flock committed to his care, but may even rejoice in the increase of a good flock." Leadership that does not include listening and responding is indeed damaging—it is quite easy to give practical examples. Benedict relates listening well and responsive leadership to *growth,* and a *good* flock with *joy.*

Clearly, this is not first and exclusively about quantitative growth. We can easily imagine a monastery in which in a few decades for various reasons the number of monks has been cut in half, and of which it could still be said that the community has *grown* in a very different sense. For the abbot must adapt and suit himself to the disposition and nature of the brothers, but that does not mean that he accepts everything he finds without critique. By a mild goodness, reproval, power of persuasion, and other forms of response he should stimulate the souls of those who are entrusted to him toward a growth process, by daily *conversio morum.* That is hard and difficult, but if it succeeds—with falling and getting up on both sides—such growth can indeed be a source of *joy.* Here also it is not difficult to adduce practical examples of Benedict's theory of good leadership. Who cannot imagine the joy of the teacher who knows how to gradually stimulate a troublemaker in class and a bungler in his work toward growth, so that he learns to realize that he has more going for him, so that he finds pleasure in exact work and is infected by his teacher's intellectual passion?

There is none too much "auscultation" needed to decide that a student is a potential troublemaker and bungler, but so much the more to discover where lie his possibilities for growth. How much persistence and attention is needed to give an adequate response in such cases? In the same class there are so many other brothers and sisters. Anyway, the remarkable thing is that such a process and its results mutually strengthen each other, so that, in a sense, it is going "by itself." I am thinking of my first principal, not a great "manager" (she had excellent co-principals) and not at all saintly, but without forcing herself and without knowing Benedict's *Rule,* who in the half-hour before the lessons started little conversations in the teachers' room and therefore knew quite precisely where lay the interests, passions, and problems, and frequently knew how to give a stimulating response. "Did you go to hear the *Fourth* by Bruckner? What a beautiful start with those four horns! You are also busy with the keyboard, aren't you?" No, not really—but it was for me a stimulant to get busy with it again. Or to another young colleague, who struggled with big problems of keeping order: "With Mr. Verhoeven"—an erudite classical scholar who had gradually become quite "prestigious"—"they used to dance on the tables." A little insight that turned out to be helpful!

Her successor—who had many management qualities and a better developed financial insight—was not seen in the teachers' room in the morning, wasting time, talking about Bruckner or Marguerite Yourcenar, and the population at that early hour shrank to those who needed to be there, who could not do anything else because of transportation problems. Many organizational processes indeed became better streamlined, but his unmistakable commitment did not come from the heart. In confidential conversation he used to sigh: "I just have to put up with these people in the manner in which things have developed." This conclusion was correct, but the implicit wish that he would have preferred to deal with other people with different habits and mentalities—a form of internal walking away—would have made Benedict shake his head. The abbot needs to adapt himself in order that he might stimulate his people toward growth! The new principal left after six rather sour years, hopefully to a place where he could grow, and his new community with him.

In the contacts which I gradually made in a later position, with people who bear extra responsibilities in business, the Church, and the community, I saw Benedict's vision of leadership confirmed again and again. Flexibility, a great capacity for adaptation to the various "natures" and dispositions of people around him, stimulating them personally toward growth, a sincere cheerfulness from the heart (even in reversals or serious illness), admitting without embarrassment that we can learn from our mistakes ("the other person might be right")—all of this stimulates toward growth, whether in a construction firm listed on the stock exchange, an orchestra, or a diocese. Where it stagnates, where it goes wrong, where distrust, intrigue, and anxiety run rampant, there is always a leader confirming Benedict's vision *ex negativo.*

Those who bear extra responsibility for others also bear extra responsibility for themselves:

> Let him know, then, that he who has undertaken the government of souls must prepare himself to render an account of them. Whatever number of brethren he knows he has under his care, he may be sure beyond doubt that on Judgment Day he will have to give the Lord an account of all these souls, as well as of his own soul (2.37-38, p. 12).

"As well of his own soul"—Benedict points here to the importance of good "maintenance" of the abbot's own soul. People need orientation and "leading" from sources outside themselves. That is true for the abbot as well. He also needs to remain in contact with sources of value that can orient him. But in practice it is often true that as one has more souls to lead, the maintenance of one's own soul is proportionately neglected.

The school principal is too busy to study in his specialty. The minister has no time anymore for his weekly walking club. The bishop has such an overloaded schedule of meetings that reading a book of poetry is cut out of his schedule. Such extra frills are often the first to be eliminated when someone accepts a position with final responsibility. But this frill is not a luxury and really not a frill either! We could go a step beyond Benedict: it is not so much the case that one's own soul "is involved," but that the feeding and maintenance of one's own soul goes along with the ability to lead other souls. We pointed out in the previous chapter the vital importance of remaining in contact with sources of value. That is true in *optima forma* for those who wish to set souls in motion. In the following fragment it is demanded of the abbot that he needs to be so familiar with the Scriptures that he can highlight the familiar parts of it to the community, but can also pass along new insights:

> Once he has been constituted, let the Abbot always bear in mind what a burden he has undertaken and to whom he will have to give an account of his stewardship and let him know that his duty is rather to profit his brethren than to preside over them. He must therefore be learned in the divine law, that he may have a treasure of knowledge from which to bring forth new things and old (64, p. 90).

According to Benedict, private study and *lectio divina* is related to the *serving* of the leader. It is indeed a salutary service when the leader, bishop, director, or chairman of a council is able to show the familiar in a new light, or is able to make the experiences and insights from very different areas fruitful in the domain where he bears responsibility.

The following fragment underscores once more that for the community a fruitful handling of human resources is related to the humanity and growth possibilities of the abbot himself:

> He must be chaste, sober and merciful. Let him exalt mercy above judgment, that he himself may obtain mercy. He should hate vices; he should love the brethren. In administering correction, he should act prudently and not go to excess, lest in seeking too eagerly to scrape off the rust he break the vessel. Let him keep his own frailty ever before his eyes and remember that the bruised reed must not be broken. By this we do not mean that he should allow vices to grow; on the contrary, as we have already said, he should eradicate them prudently and with charity, in a way which may seem best in each case. Let him study rather to be loved than to be feared. Let him not be excitable and worried, nor exacting and headstrong, nor jealous and over-suspicious; for then he is never at rest.

> In his commands let him be prudent and considerate . . . let him be discreet and moderate. . . . . Taking this, then, and other examples of discretion, the mother of virtues, let him so temper all things that the strong may have something to strive after, and the weak may not fall back in dismay (64.7-19, pp. 90, 91).

This somewhat longer fragment from the *Rule* may at first glance appear quite good and pious. But on closer investigation we again discover valuable advice for good leadership.

First, there is the aspect of *example:* chastity, moderation, mercy, quiet leading, reflection. Students, coworkers, members of an orchestra, diocesans: all have excellent noses to measure the distance between what the leader *stands for* and what he himself *is.* The greater the distance, the less people are inclined to take seriously what is coming from "higher up"—for they see that the leader does not believe in it himself. The results are loss of trust and motivation. And when things are going exceptionally well in an organization, one often sees people at the top where the distance between the leader and the people he leads is minimal or even absent. The teacher who takes his subject very seriously (the scientific, pedagogical, and didactic aspects), is also taken seriously by his students—that is the secret of "natural respect." In other fields the situation is similar. Some directors just *are* music, one is bound to be inspired by it. Now and again someone who is leading the liturgy calls forth a response within you: this has to be *true*—and I must *change* my life.

An anecdote: after a festive and warm celebration of the liturgy in a family circle, an agnostic, probably unchurched cousin came to me quite shocked, offering the observation: "It seems to me that this priest really believes in what he says!" With these words he unconsciously indicated how exceptional that seemed to him.

The relative rarity of this situation makes us recognize the problem. Precisely the people with whom it seems to go "by itself" are the ones who have studied intensively, for years, cultivating, practicing—and they will be the first to tell you that it never goes "by itself."

The *Rule* also sums up some qualities an abbot should *not* have: hurry, fear, stubbornness, jealousy, suspicion—"for then he is never at rest." And his turmoil multiplies, doing damage to the community. The fact that Benedict mentions these things makes one suspect that he knew that quite a few leaders show one or more of these qualities (and they are easily combined!).

To be sure, they are all damaging: hurry is synonymous with making mistakes, fear makes us tense, stubbornness puts the brakes on flexibility, jealousy sours the organizations, suspicion naturally calls forth reactions which in turn confirm and strengthen suspicion. Where something is askew in an organization, Benedict's catalogue is a useful checklist. The complementary positive list speaks for itself: rest stimulates careful work; cheerfulness kept down to earth by realism can stimulate others to remove the barriers of their own anxieties; openness to other solutions beside your own enriches decision-making; experiencing pleasure from the good accomplishments of others—and expressing that as well—stimulates others to show that there is more going on in them; a basic attitude of trust may even tempt the grumblers and troublemakers not to shame such trust.

The cited fragment also contains some useful tips for thoughtful human resource management. First, concerning the brothers who need to be corrected. To begin with, it needs to be done and in a timely manner. This rule is both logical and difficult. Often one knows that something should be said or that action is needed, but then one needs to conquer one's own barrier, and besides, hope that it may succeed. It does not work. Poor quality multiplies and strengthens (as does the presence of quality) and quickly a situation arises that can only be corrected with difficulty. As a young teacher, I was advised by my first principal to intervene *immediately* in class, even with the smallest event that might be harmful, and to be consistent. I followed his advice in all classes but one—from my conceited lust for experimenting, I am afraid. In the other classes I was very strict, sometimes rather exaggeratedly I thought, but the students worked, we knew where we stood, and gradually I could loosen the reins somewhat and we became a bit more relaxed (I especially) and our attention was increasingly oriented to the subject. In the one "experimental class" everyone was immediately relaxed and pleasant, after a short time very pleasant, the students were busy with everything except what was on my program, and after a few months almost brute force was needed to turn the situation around.

Another logical but still more difficult piece of advice by Benedict: "To hate the wrong, but to love the brothers." It can be most salutary for a coworker when he experiences, after a mistake and a corrective reprimand, that he regains trust, and from the heart. And then the past is not opened again, not even indirectly or between the lines. Such an approach stimulates new growth. But the practice is often different. One, two mistakes, and some leaders begin to create a file which may come in handy at some future time, when one wants to get rid of that coworker. Even more: the leader may as it were be on the lookout for new mistakes, and in such a climate of suspicion and distrust, new transgressions are easily seen. Suspicious behavior of little bosses injects poison into the organization; however, correction directed toward "the good" and which expresses hearty confidence in a better future quality, acts as an interhuman elixir. In connection with the correction of brothers, Benedict points out to the abbot his own fragility and frailty. For the leadership of the abbot will also be a way of falling and getting up again; his own path will be helped on a daily basis with a constantly renewable moral quality (the promise of the *conversio morum*). The abbot also may be wounded and healed by his brothers.

In this connection, one might point to an omission in Benedict's *Rule:* so much is expected and demanded of the abbot, but who cares for *his* soul? First of all the brothers, for whom the *ausculta* is also valid in this sense, that they need to be alert for signals that the abbot needs support and warmth. In an atmosphere of attentive benevolence in an organization, the leadership and the charisma of the abbot may grow.

You may approach your new principal, conductor, or bishop with suspicion and distrust—and things affirming this suspicion and mistrust happen automatically. But you can also welcome them with trust and offer them much benevolent space in the beginning phase. Authority may be *granted* someone. Charisma then becomes a *double* gift.

A position with final responsibility is often associated with loneliness: it's lonely at the top. That risk is indeed present. And this is not only because distance between abbot and brothers inadvertently grows, or because important decisions, after consultation with all, must ultimately be made by one person. The loneliness of the ultimately responsible person also has to do with his time management and the lack of persons who might correct him. We shall return to time management in the following chapter.

We have already indicated in this connection that occupying a high position is often accompanied with stopping—because of time pressure—the maintenance of one's own soul, and keeping recreational contacts at a low key: the walking club, the weekly tennis night, choir practice, an evening of playing chess, and relaxed chatting with a good friend. Not only is this shrinking schedule damaging for one's own soul, but also for the quality of leadership. It is good to stay in a "safe zone" (Cornelis Verhoeven's term, in his concise description of friendship) on a regular basis, where you need not watch your words, in which you can relax with people who are not in any way hierarchically related to you. Such a safe zone needs to be cultivated. A bishop, a captain of industry, a minister or an abbot needs a small group of friends who might meet monthly, bringing a bottle of wine, coming to visit and with their feet on the table can talk and laugh about *anything*. In such a situation, the bishop may without risk lay his cares and uncertainties on the table, and his friends can honestly and in good humor correct the bishop when he has made some unnuanced and rash pronouncements in the press. The abbot also needs the *correctio fraterna,* the brotherly correction.

The cited fragment also clarifies that the *correctio* by the abbot must in the first place be brotherly. Exaggerated correction threatens the integrity of the brother. Vices need to be rooted out—it sounds paradoxical—"prudently and with charity." That is to say, "in the way which may seem best in each case"—in correction also, the capacity to adapt and to be flexible is expected of the abbot. An *identical* measure of punishment is *wrong* punishment in this connection—this is about a measure of correction that does optimal justice to the possibilities for conversion and healing for every brother individually.

For Benedict, leadership is clearly a question of "moderation." On the other hand, there are ways of leadership that are "immoderate." In such cases the leader is suffocatingly present, is immediately on top of things, hastily and sloppily cuts (often the wrong) knots in an overbearing manner; in short, he meddles with everything and everyone. Benedict's emphasis is very different; he uses words like "circumspect," "reflective," "with a sense of moderation." With this circumspection and reflection also belongs the ability to distinguish between situations in which one clearly needs to be present and others where it is prudent to take a step back, to respect the others' ability to correct and manage themselves. Additionally, sometimes it may be wiser not to personally intervene and correct, but to search out sensible people who have a good relationship with the persons in question and from whom advice and correction is liable to be more heartily accepted than from the man on the top. At the end of the selected fragment about the abbot, almost as an unnoticed bonus, there is some advice which, if it were really taken seriously by leaders, might perhaps be the litmus test for growth and flourishing of an organization: the abbot "must temper all things *that the strong may have something to strive after, and the weak may not fall back in dismay.*" Catherine Wybourne translates: "that the strong have something still to wish for and the weak nothing from which to shrink." "To shrink" perhaps shows better the relationship to the context of growth and development; "to shrink" does not only mean "recoil" but also "(cause) to crimp," "diminish," "shrivel." Good leadership includes stimulating people toward *optimal*, not toward maximal performance. This is about making an appeal to people, so that they arrive at a level of performance that optimally *fits them*. One might approach the weaker ones in the organization in such a manner that they shrink some more and recoil before forms of response they would be incapable of. There is a certain tendency among leaders to focus, particularly with the weaker ones, on things they cannot do (anymore), in what fails and goes wrong. It would be unrealistic and bad for the community to close one's eyes to this. However, a fixation on mistakes and the demanding of what is (no longer) possible is just as harmful. It is fruitful to investigate what does belong to someone's possibilities and to see whether strengthening and growth is possible in that area. An illustration from the monastic world: an older monk who has difficulty walking is, of course, no longer assigned to serve tables (though everyone takes a turn, even the abbot); but if this monk happens to have a good voice, he more often gets a turn reading at meals. It should not be difficult to think of nonmonastic variants.

But not only should the weak be prevented from shrinking back and pining away; it is just as important that there is something for the strong to look forward to. This is easily forgotten. Leaders spend much of their time on weaker brothers and departments, on problem cases and grumblers. This attention is needed. But just as much attention should be devoted to the strong and successful, of whom it is wrongly thought that they can take care of themselves. That is only true in a superficial sense, and only in the short run. A lack of attentive appreciation and a lack of challenges in one's own organization may quickly result in the search for challenges elsewhere. It is simply a matter of good human resource management to keep a finger on the pulse of the strong brothers as well. How could they still grow? Is there a talent that is insufficiently tapped? Which supplemental formation programs might promote their growth? Though not at all burned out or tired, do they perhaps need a study or recreational leave?

Again, this is about the art of good listening. An additional difficulty is that the strong and the weak appear mostly *mixed*. Much capacity to distinguish is needed to get a good view of the situation and as leader to give the right response. However, the leader who has an ear for the signals of intellectual, practical, artistic, moral, and other spiritual talents and growth potential, addresses these opportunities for growth and cultivates them, all of which certainly contribute to the flourishing of his organization.

There is a beautiful illustration of this attitude in a Belgian software company, where someone apparently spontaneously had himself thought of these obvious ideas of Benedict and had done something about them. The top boss of the company had two bright ideas that look very much like what has just been discussed.

First it was decided that *everyone* in the company, from the porter to the boss himself, would have a (paid) study day every two weeks. Quite remarkably, everyone was free to fill in their time as they wished, as long as they could show they had studied. The programmers did not need to feel obligated to enlarge their professional knowledge; they were doing that spontaneously. Someone began taking a course in art history; another took a year's course in icon painting; someone else took violin lessons. The porter did not need to take a course on first aid or security, but might also study Spanish if he wished, to get along better on his vacation, or a course in creative writing. Colleagues from the same sector shook their heads at this innovation: 10 percent less work time, more expense, no obligatory "useful" training. The result after one year: considerably better (financial) results, less turnover, more work satisfaction.

The second measure looked just as strange: the company decided, when vacancies occurred, to hire a fixed percentage of new employees *over* fifty years old, in all regions, while there is a search elsewhere for ways to get rid of older employees in the best way possible. The motivation for this measure: these new, but older coworkers moved slower in certain respects, but brought experience and a kind of stability. The new chair of the cleaning crew was fifty-three in a group of mostly twenty-some-year-olds. She appeared to be a secure beacon in the surf; she enjoyed more respect and trust than if she had been of the same age or just a little older than the rest, and she noted quicker when something was going on in the group. The new director of innovation management was fifty-five; he could hardly keep up with the young men and women of his division, mostly twenty-five to thirty years younger, with their newer ideas. But through his experience he had built a capacity to see which ideas were viable and which were not. He too brought rest through his company; moreover he was no threat in terms of possibilities for promotion of the "young and coming" men, because he could only stay a few more years. This measure appeared to be fruitful as well. Both are quality impulses of a (probably unknown) Benedictine allure: a software company with a good abbot.

The good abbot is also the one who keeps the community going and who has the vision in which way that might lead, with the openness toward sources of orientation in their own community. This is indeed about keeping the *community* going, whereby the main thing is not to see who walks the fastest, but that everyone walks. Even the coals which almost appear to have been extinguished he needs to revive with suitable care. But also, the fire of those who fully burn are constantly in need of fuel. Leadership is difficult and demanding—but the abbot does not have to do everything by himself. There is more mastery to be found that may be utilized in the community.

3. *The Person of the Cellarer: "A Man for All Seasons"* [2]

The cellarer of the monastery, now mostly called the "economist," has (partial) responsibility for the material things of the monastery. In modern jargon: together with a few others, he is part of the management team of the abbey. Benedict devotes a separate chapter to the cellarer in his *Rule,* another chapter which can easily be translated for the world outside of the monastery. Just as with the abbot, Benedict does not begin with a summation of tasks and qualifications, but with a description of the *personal traits* of a suitable cellarer.

> As cellarer of the monastery let there be chosen from the community one who is wise, of mature character, sober, not a great eater, not haughty, not excitable, not offensive, not slow, not wasteful, but a God-fearing man who may be like a father to the whole community (ch. 31, p. 48).

Again, *fatherhood* is emphasized—apparently that is a mark of good leadership, whether applicable for the ultimate responsibility or to one of the other managers.

---

[2] Much of the information in this paragraph relies on: Anselm Grün, *Menschen führen—Leben wecken. Anregungen aus der Regel Benedikts.* Münsterscharzach, 1998. This is a beautiful monograph concerning the relevant chapter of Benedict's *Rule,* written from the author's own experience as cellarer (and abbot).

The fragment begins with a few positive traits. The leader needs to be *wise*. The Latin is *sapiens,* from *sapere,* a verb related to "tasting" or "taste." *Sapientia* is a form of knowing that differs from *scientia* which is the certain knowledge of simple things that may be understood and argued. *Sapientia* has to do with the art of judging what is complex, just as someone with taste can properly evaluate a complicated dish. Taste is also about the art of making the right choice in complicated matters.

The leader needs also to be "tested" in the sense that his character has matured with falling and getting up again. A boy wonder who has only successes to his account we want to wish well, but would he be a good leader?

The cellarer must be sober, *sobrius;* that is, a sobriety going beyond drinking too much. Sobriety is also thoughtfulness, the ability to have a sober view on reality. The moderation of the cellarer also means that he should not cram himself full of other things, not the purely material. Those who find themselves in a leadership position can also "cram themselves full" in other ways: only wanting to sleep in five-star hotels, arranging exorbitant salaries and options, or thinking that you need to sit in the first row.

There are also some instructive *negative* descriptions, especially what the manager must *not* be. Benedict would not have mentioned these things if he had not known that in practice these do characterize many leaders. Not haughty—*non elatus.* One of the temptations of leadership is to negate and forget one's own fragility so that one becomes proud, in a beautiful German word: *hochnäsig,* "with the nose high up" [in the air]; in English: stuck-up or conceited. Conceit implies that one does not want to learn and listen anymore; it may be the fundamental flaw of failing leaders.

The cellarer should not be fickle: *non turbulentus.* Decisive leadership is often thought of as being about shaking up things or creating turbulence. That might raise dust and cause a lot of noise *(turba),* but this is only non-oriented unrest, leadership that is unclear and without any perspective. Yet bustle and excitement is frequently associated with decisive leadership. Practice teaches us that unrest is coupled with a lack of effectiveness, while on the other hand rest and strength are almost synonymous.

Not offensive or grim—*non iniuriosus*. Being offensive and rough offend coworkers, an offense which multiplies in the organization and which will not be forgotten by those affected by it. It is a misconception that one keeps people sharp by jumping on their mistakes and snapping at them. They will shrink back and crawl into their shells but from within their shells they will find effective ways to take revenge. We will return to this subject.

The cellarer should not be slow—*non tardus*. Fickle turbulence with its appearance of dynamism goes well with slowness, with extraordinarily hesitant leadership: giving no response to repeated questions, a behavior of postponement ("this is not yet on our schedule," "I will get back to that"); because of the total lack of long-term planning, such a person never tackles anything, is late *(tardus)* everywhere because of too many appointments and keeps dawdling. Superficial quickness and inner slowness can easily be combined.

Not wasteful—*non prodigus*. The verb "to spoil" well portrays the idea of wastefulness. It is being wasteful which is also spoiling and decaying. The wasteful manager spoils not only money and other things, but also sets a process of decay in motion, as relationships begin to shift and to rot, and people feel "rotten" with such management.

This series of negative personal characteristics has a simple complement: to be "God-fearing." This is a term which may be misunderstood, as if the cellarer must work anxiously and all too scrupulously, bent under the strict glance of the highest authority. A [Dutch] dictionary describes "God-fearing" in a way that leaves out anxiety: "filled with awe and respect toward God." "Awe" and "respect" are also the main meanings of "fear"; an "anxious feeling that something is threatening" is only the secondary meaning. What Benedict wants to express by "God-fearing" is that the cellarer's spirituality must penetrate his (mostly of an everyday variety) work. Such awe and respect must color his fundamental attitude, also in the context of tools, supplies, turnover, and bookkeeping. A fundamental attitude of awe and respect certainly cannot be reconciled with wastefulness, slowness, offensiveness, fickleness, and haughti-ness. Respect is also related to attention, when all the antennas are out to pick up signals calling for a response, looking for possibilities for quality improvement.

> Let him have charge of everything. He shall do nothing without the Abbot's orders, but keep to his instructions. Let him not vex the brethren. If any brother happens to make some unreason-able demand of him, instead of vexing the brother with a contemptuous refusal he should humbly give the reason for denying the improper request (ch. 31, p. 49).

The cellarer has a delegated responsibility. He cares for the daily management of *everything* in the monastery, while listen-ing attentively to the one who bears the ultimate responsibility. The community and the organization are not served well when middle management goes its own way, no longer directed to what is advantageous for the whole. But in addition to the awe and respect he bears toward the abbot, the cellarer also needs to treat the brothers with awe and respect when they ask some-thing of him or wish to speak to him, even if they ask for some-thing unreasonable. Benedict undoubtedly knew, as we do, the often occurring situation when people who are low on the totem pole are inclined to act in a rather obedient and slimy fashion toward those who are "above" them (while protecting their own turf as much as possible) and act from their height toward those "below" them with a growl and snarl. Both atti-tudes are disastrous for living and working together. Particu-larly the "offending" of brothers acts like a shovel of sand in a running machine. There is a direct relationship between non-genuine and grieving treatment and sick leave. In addition to sick leave, the offended coworker has other possibilities of "revenge": to stall things, attract others to grumble with him, do half-work, "forget" appointments and other forms of inter-nal forgetting. The results of this infection of "offending" is very costly, even financially. Anselm Grün in his book about the cellarer cites the example of General Motors, which in 1995 spent more money on absenteeism and other "health problems" than on their purchase of steel. But there are other results as well: in an organization where an unfriendly climate rules internally by offended behavior, with ever more "winners" and "losers" in the power relations, one would not want to commit oneself forever. That means much turnover, the need for temporary workers, and expensive training of new personnel.

One of the reasons for internal lack of peace in an organization is unclear argumentation or the lack of it surrounding decisions and management plans. Benedict emphasizes that when it is necessary for the cellarer to say "no" it should be done in a sober and sensible manner; this need not come across as arbitrariness, but defended instead by means of lucid reasons. The same is true when the cellarer says "yes."

The demanding task of the cellarer, as we saw earlier with the abbot, requires attention for his own soul, and beyond that attention for the souls entrusted to him.

> Let him keep guard over his own soul, mindful always of the Apostle's saying that "he who has ministered well acquires for himself a good standing." Let him take the greatest care of the sick, of children, of guests and of the poor, knowing without doubt that he will have to render an account for all these on the Day of Judgment.

Again, the point is valid that those who take good care of their own souls can help move the souls of others. From an inner rest one is better able to call forth quality in others, more than when one is rushed and not oriented properly.

Giving leadership is a spiritual matter. In the words of Anselm Grün: "To lead means first of all to arouse people to life, to entice life out of them. Leading is the art of finding the key which can open the treasury of your co-worker." Leading is education, an educative leading out *(educare)*, to tempt people to arrive at maturity, to grow in their tasks, so that they find pleasure, that their little soul becomes a real soul. That *everything* must be pervaded by the right *spirit* is beautifully expressed in the following verses from the chapter on the cellarer:

> Let him regard all the utensils of the monastery and its whole property as if they were the sacred vessels of the altar. Let him not think that he may neglect anything.

There is no dividing line between the holy (the service of the altar) and simple work (washing dishes). The service of the altar would lose spiritual quality if housekeeping were neglected. The housekeeping flourishes the more as the service of the altar is cultivated more respectfully. In a climate of "neglect *nothing*" (the building well painted, beautiful tools, the conditions of the toilets, the neatness of the service automobiles, the legibility of the annual report, a tastefully designed business facility—the list may be extended indefinitely) the value of everything comes into focus and the organization radiates the message that a good *spirit* dominates there. But that would not be genuine if the service of the altar were not appropriately cultivated: offering opportunity for reflection and study; celebrating successes; taking festival days seriously; a few days of silence with the management team to create time for culture and quiet consultation. The elements contained in the following paragraph may also be translated into daily life:

> He should neither be a miser nor a prodigal and squanderer of the monastery's substance, but should do all things with measure and in accordance with the Abbot's instructions. Above all things let him have humility; and if he has nothing else to give let him give a good word in answer, for it is written, "A good word is above the best gift." Let him have under his care all that the Abbot has assigned to him, but not presume to deal with what he has forbidden him (ch. 31, pp. 49, 50).

In part, this repeats earlier guidelines: do not be wasteful, his relationship to the abbot and the abbot's final responsibility, a sense of moderation. New elements are "humility" and the importance of a good and friendly word. The word "humility" can even easier call forth misunderstanding than the term "God-fearing." When we think of piety, we think of ignoring oneself, making and keeping oneself small. But that would be a lack of respect for one's own worth and integrity. Something else is indicated by *humilitas:* it is an admonishing reminder as to who is the leader, of his own earthiness and frailty. From that perspective one becomes conscious of someone else's weakness, seeing it in a different light. That may subsequently be a stimulus to deal with courtesy to others. A climate of courtesy and respect in the contact between leaders and coworkers functions like balm in an organization, just like rudeness and caprice inject poison into it. Just like a wrongly chosen and offensive word can make people shrivel and become paralyzed—Anselm Grün calls this "spiritual environmental pollution" [geistige Umweltverschmutzung]—a good and friendly word can raise up people and make them flourish. Again, this is about an attitude of the leader requiring much *discretio* and attention, and an adequate response to noted signals.

> Let him give the brethren their appointed allowance of food without any arrogance or delay, that they may not be scandalized, mindful of the Word of God as to what he deserves "who shall scandalize one of the little ones."
>
> If the community is a large one, let helpers be given him, that by their assistance he may fulfill with a quiet mind the office committed to him. The proper times should be observed in giving the things that have to be given and asking for the things that have to be asked for, that no one may be troubled or vexed in the house of God (ch. 31, p. 50).

It almost sounds like a litany: no pride, no slowness, giving no occasion for discontent, supply what is needed, being on time—how many supervisors have the inclination to give a little less than what is needed, and preferably late? Benedict states, by contrast: do not offend, do not set traps for your coworkers, promote their peace of mind. But a new element is added: the importance of obtaining assistance on time when your task becomes too voluminous. Else, the equanimity of the leader is endangered, with all the bad results of this. Sloppy, hurried, fragmented leadership is sin in many respects. The one who is ultimately responsible, who sees the signals of overloading in his coworkers, but because of frugality does not respond adequately, is penny wise and pound foolish.

In this fragment the abbey is called "house of God" [*domus Dei*]. One might consider this name for every "house" that wants to be a good place for living and working together, a place where things and people flourish. Such an attitude may also be meaningful for those who do not share Benedict's context of faith. It is like the anecdote about the lucky horseshoe and the physicists Einstein and Bohr mentioned in the introduction of this book: but it works to lead your organization as a *domus Dei,* with the leader as steward—*oikonomos* in Greek. Benedictine leadership is *economical* in a fundamental sense.

PART IV

Benedictine Time Management: A Full Agenda, but Never Busy

Living in a Wholesome Rhythm

In the first chapter, based on my first acquaintance with Benedictine life, I discussed my first lessons in the Benedictine way with time: the wholesome rhythm of an ordered division of the day; the bell which keeps indicating that something needs to be begun or that it is time to quit something; an attitude which is not so much directed to "finishing" a job as it is to the work itself; and the taking seriously of the periods of concentration and relaxation. Each of these elements is briefly highlighted in this chapter. The paradoxical conclusion is that in a Benedictine dealing with time, one's agenda is *totally* filled but that one is *never* busy.

As with other Benedictine quality rules we need to point out that there should be a considerable distance between the consciousness of the correct attitude and its realization. Monks and nuns can become overwrought; people also hurry in monasteries. I prepared many a lecture about Benedictine life under pressure of time and in reasonably "stressed" circumstances. But that does not dispel the idea that it is good to remind oneself now and then that it is also possible to do things differently, and that one can take realistic little steps in the right direction.

This will indeed have to deal with *little steps* as always in processes that may be labeled *conversio morum*. Suddenly everything is totally different—such a step cannot be taken. Bad habits relating to going and standing *in time* can only gradually and with much falling and getting up again develop toward a better and more wholesome attitude. Good habits must indeed be *practiced,* as when someone with a tough determination daily reserves a half-hour for practicing his musical instrument independently of what he feels like or giving in to tempting alternatives. Daily progress will be minimal but after a year even the musical layperson can see the fruits. Such tough determination is again a question of *stabilitas.*

The little steps toward better time management need to be *realistic.* The copying of the rhythm of the abbey with six or seven daily times of prayer, a few hours of *lectio divina,* fixed recreation periods, etc., in a reasonably demanding business life or in a family—that is unrealistic and produces only frustration. This is about finding a rhythm that fits you. One needs to be like a good abbot for oneself: not making any demands that will destroy you, but on the other hand put the bar high enough so that there is a daily challenge.

An essential step forward is the development of a fitting order of the day: a division of the day that gives a rhythm to the day, with a reasonably fixed pattern of exertion and relaxation, of spiritual breathing in and breathing out, of ordering one's environment and moments when one is in touch with something beautiful.[1] Such an order of the day, which will differ for everyone, is at the same time beneficial for everyone: for the active professional and for the retired, for the student and for the disabled, for the househusband and for the bishop, for the graduate student with a pressing deadline, and for the professor on a sabbatical. This last item may appear remarkable, but from my own experience and that of others I know that such a period of free study and relaxing recreation may also be frustrating and may fruitlessly slip through one's fingers un-

---

[1] On the beneficial result of the monastic order of the day and its translation into everyday life, my brother and fellow-oblate Geert A. M. Derkse wrote the article "Benedictijns leven: Het nu anders beleven," [Benedictine Life: Experiencing the Now Differently] in: *Verbum* 66 (1999) 7–8, pp. 144–50.

less one structures one's day in a manner befitting to the situation. *Befitting* is always essential and when one does not live and work together with brothers and sisters who live by the same rhythm—which is the case for most of us—daily accommodations will be unavoidable and appropriate. When I gradually began to want to live by the rhythm of the abbey, from a distance as it were and in a suitable form, I was too rigid initially. In the monastery, the day is closed fifteen minutes before nine with the Compline, and I also wanted to follow this schedule from a distance. But there were repeatedly days when I, because of meetings, lectures, and other circumstances, was quite busy with very different things at that time. That did not only produce a slight displeasure (*murmuratio* can be caused by many things), but when I later arrived home I did not take another fifteen minutes to close the day in a quiet manner—until I once visited a small group of monks in Sweden. In their guestroom I found an order of the day as well. But I noted that they dealt with order flexibly. All three of them also had outside obligations. But they started their day at the same time and they also closed it at the same time. One afternoon I rode with one of them, the prior, to a benefit concert in a castle some distance away. There was a reception afterward. Back home the other two had waited for us. The time for the Compline was already past, so I suspected that we needed to hurry to the little chapel. But the prior pulled some chairs together on the veranda, treated us to a beer and we spoke about the concert. After that we sang the Compline. When I later commented on this, the prior said: "The time of the Compline is quite flexible with us, but we always sing it." Order with flexibility: that is typically Benedictine.

Within the rhythm of such a flexible order there are four essential skills to be practiced: the art of beginning, the art of quitting, the art of the right attitude between beginning and quitting, and the art to keep a respectful attitude toward the "seasons" of the day.[2]

---

[2] This term and its related ideas are based on the beautiful little book by David Steindl-Rast, O.S.B., *De muziek van de stilte. Een dag uit het kloosterleven* [The Music of the Silence. A Day in the Life of the Monastery]. Utrecht, 1996.

THE ART OF BEGINNING

In his *Rule* Benedict emphasizes a number of times that as little as possible distance should exist between appeal and response. The greater the distance, the less adequate may be the response. Attentive listening and responding should go as it were from one to the other in one smooth movement, without internal and external hesitation and muttering. The word heard leads immediately to the corresponding deed. When the prayer bell is sounded, you put your work down. Without lingering, but with dignity you hasten to the chapel. The same is valid for each moment of the order of the day: the beginning of meals, the beginning of recreation, the beginning of work. The fact that Benedict so often underscores the importance of responding immediately is undoubtedly related to his (and our) experience that a true *beginning* is difficult. When we need to start with a chore we find difficult or annoying, we are often exceptionally clever at postponing it. We do many things with much superficial show of dynamism and busyness—we telephone, answer e-mails, set up schemes for the following week, sending a quick fax, meeting—all except really starting with that particular task! It is quite possible to spend the entire day in the office or at your workbench or at home, diligently, living out all sorts of postponement behavior, and even be tired in the evening, but without really having worked for a minute. And even when the item that should have had your attention long before you lie down, there are again subtler forms of pseudo-activity by which you again *fail* to respond to what is being asked of you. Externally you have conformed yourself to "the bell" but internally you have not started at all.

Benedictine beginning is external and internal beginning as soon "as the bell is sounded," immediately stepping into the activity (or recreation or whatever is on the schedule) at the stated time and to practice signaling and eliminating every postponement behavior, no matter how subtle. This is all just as obvious as difficult. But with practice and persistence the distance between the "bell" and the real beginning can gradually diminish. First, dawdling and hesitating, "I should start" because "it is time after all," but gradually that may change into the good habit of getting up when the starting signal has been given. External conforming to a bell can become an internal habit.

I saw a good illustration of immediately responding to what "lies before you" in a TV interview with the singer Dietrich Fischer-Diskau. He always acts in a quiet and concentrated manner, as could be seen in the care he took answering questions in an interview. However, now and then the interviewer played a musical fragment. When that happened, the singer immediately assumed a different attitude, lowered his head a little as if he were looking inside, and was immediately absorbed *in* the music—as if someone (he!) turned a knob. He immediately *became* music. He was immediately in contact with a life-source of value. That is Benedictine beginning.

Real beginning may be difficult with a substantial chore, but this point may be extended to little things. You see small signals which really demand a quick response. But you postpone them. "I'll look at it tomorrow, it is only a small thing." Often you forget, or tomorrow you postpone it again and before you know it is no longer something small. Every day offers possibilities for small but quick "mini-responses" by which you can straighten out something, give a look of appreciation or a small push in the right direction. Alertness is needed to tackle these little things *(ausculta)*, a good capacity of distinction to determine whether a response is urgently needed and possible, and a committed readiness to react as quickly as possible—*conversio* on a small scale.

Even this small *conversio* is difficult; we prefer to look the other way. But these small denials, this small failure to begin—they are bad for the soul. One may drag along a track of countless little missed chances that may become more damaging and oppressive than one might expect for something that is but small. Using an old word: this is *sin*. On the other hand, by exercise one can nurture the habit to give where possible and fitting, an immediate response and from the heart. Even on the microlevel—again an old word—*sanctification* is possible.

THE ART OF QUITTING

Beginning is difficult, but so is quitting. That is first of all true in a purely chronological sense. Particularly when you bear extra responsibility and you have many things on your plate, there is the understandable inclination not to take a break and to keep working. That may appear responsible, but it is not. To keep on going is almost synonymous with "making mistakes." Moreover, one is not to take away the moments of rest and recreation which are needed to remain fresh and lively.

It is not only an overcrowded agenda which might tempt one to keep on going, but also simply that it is just going so well. It might call forth irritation, dawdling (but of a different kind this time), and grumbling because "the bell" says that it is time for the afternoon walk or some beautiful music in the evening. But the positive work also must be stopped on time. Experienced writers and composers know that one needs to stop just when one has the feeling that one could keep going for quite some time and not just when one feels tired and worn out.

Quitting is also difficult in a more psychological sense. One might, in an internal sense, conform to the appeal of the bell and put down one's work because it is time for recreation, but internally one keeps plenty busy. To be sure, the much-too-long meeting is over but when you return home you are still busy with it. Grumbling to yourself about the stupidities of others and yourself, you ride home. That is triple *zund* [sin] as they say in the province of Brabant. To begin with, the meeting is over and you can no longer influence it one way or another; a repetition of wrong moves or a reflection of what clever or destructive things you might have wanted to say is therefore out of the question. Secondly, such sulking and grumbling rumination and forging base plans is bad for the soul. It works like an internal poison and the grouchiness that no one hears can devour you internally. Thirdly, you are not open to what your surroundings have to tell you, that would let you catch your breath.

Benedictine quitting in such a situation means to admit our consciousness of the present: I am traveling now, I ride through this beautiful landscape. Naturally, even in such an attitude, thoughts, fragments of conversation, and irritations may present themselves, but with some practice we just let that happen and at the same time do not *stay* in them (grumbling can become a true swamp) by consciously directing attention to something positive: the landscape, the skyline of the approaching city, a few beautiful lines of poetry that come to mind in this connection, sounds of birds you try to identify. Such an attitude offers a triple profit: you have ridden through a totally different world, you bring home a refreshed mind (which is more pleasant for my family than to hear me grumbling), and the next conversation is begun with fewer old hurts. By this falling and getting up again, but also with a certain toughness to keep going *(stabilitas)*, a healthy habit is nourished. First a good meeting, then turning the knob, then riding home. That may appear simple and naïve but the practice, as always, while difficult and (if maintained) creates a wholesome effect.

The example given started with quitting something negative. As said before: the positive also needs to be ended when the time has come. Not only because it is better to lay down your work with a good rather than with a squeezed-dry feeling, or actually ending the pleasant conversation during recreation at a suitable moment (before landing in the driveling stage). The most important reason to quit something in the right manner is to begin something else with the right attitude. The art of beginning and the art of quitting presuppose one another.

THE ART OF RELAXED DIGNITY BETWEEN BEGINNING AND QUITTING

Between the beginning bell and the quitting bell there is time, representing something, and there is the *attitude* in which you manage that time. Often, our attention is pretty much occupied by things outside of it. We are busy, mulling over things from the past or we begin to worry about what is coming. We have not yet begun in earnest and we are already quitting. Such an attitude is again triple *zund* [sin]: the past is over, what is yet to come needs our attention later (and does not really get it this way), and the worst is: the task before us does not get our full attention. This attitude devours energy and causes a leaching of quality. Benedictine working means first of all the turning away of attention to what is past and what is yet to come (again, *conversio*) and the call is answered by attending to what needs to be done presently (again, *conversio*). The field of

vision of attention has limited itself to the piece of time between beginning and quitting.

Something important needs to be added. Even if you succeed, with persistent practice (again, *stabilitas*) to limit the field
of vision of your attention to the task now before you, then
there is yet again the temptation to consider something else,
namely, finishing the task. At first sight, nothing appears to be
wrong with that. The job needs to be finished, the meeting
needs to be rounded off fruitfully, the bicycle must be repaired,
that contract needs to be signed! That is true enough, and
Benedict would be the last one to deny that our attentive listening is ultimately directed toward a result. But when, during
the work, the lecture and even recreation are psychologically
directed particularly toward being "finished" with it—I will be
so happy when this article is finally finished, when this unpleasant meeting will be over with, etc.—then again, the attention does not lie where it should be: with the phase of work
with which I am presently occupied. Moreover, to see its conclusion as the goal while the work is being done (which it is, of
course), the work itself does not get complete attention (which
would contribute the most to the quality of the goal); instead,
you feel your time pressure and tempo increasing to a higher
pitch than would be suitable to optimal work. That also produces loss of quality. Benedictine working—and reading, and
playing bridge during recreation, and studying a new piece of
music in your spare time—includes: beginning immediately
with what needs to be done, giving it your complete attention
(untrammeled by anything else—which it will receive later, or
has had it already), to let that attention be quiet and dignified
and—very important and very difficult—being, in a sense, un-
concerned about finishing the job. When the bell announces
that something else needs to be tackled now, you lay down one
thing (which will receive your attention again later) and you
begin something else with the same attitude. Thus, in a sense,
you are "never busy," because in a calm, continuing line as it
were, you give things your attention "one by one," including
the moments of recreation and feeding.

This appears just as unattainable as naïve and, moreover,
difficult to combine with a time which appears hectic, with a

surplus of parallel tasks and rapid possibilities for communication. However, everyone's world contains possibilities for putting something of this attitude into practice. The often favorable and accelerating communication techniques of faxes and e-mails tempt us to respond rapidly, hurriedly, and therefore inadequately, often at the expense of the work which occupied us presently, thus resulting in a double loss of quality. In my own case, when I noted that in my work as director of an organization I yielded to that temptation and began to feel more hurried and pressured, I introduced (with repeated falling back in this sin) a small form of *conversio*. Our secretary is quite capable of distinguishing which of the incoming faxes and electronic mail are really urgent enough for me to interrupt my present task. The rest gets its turn as if it were ordinary mail and that is where it is placed—in the order in which it is received, in the timeslots I reserve for my correspondence, not worrying if not everything can be finished in that time period. That has removed some unrest with me and led to some modest improvement of quality. This procedure may, however, lead to some reactions of surprise, as appears when someone calls when I do not react quickly enough to their mail. In various forms, I often have the following conversation: "Did you get my mail?" "I did." "What do you think?" "I don't know. I did not get to your letter yet, but when I do, I will have to think about it. I promise I will give your proposal the same attention as others on my desk." This is how every context offers possibilities for a more wholesome time discipline.

That also applies to the work tempo. By concentrating on what lies before you and on your next step—without rushing for a distant goal—the tempo becomes calmer. An inexperienced mountain climber often walks too fast and then needs to take a breath beside the path. The experienced mountain resident walks in a slower but constant tempo and reaches the top quicker. An acquaintance of mine once had to spade a big piece of garden and had hired a tough older man from the village to help. They began at the same time: my youthful colleague began energetically, in a solid tempo; the townsman seems to work a little slower and appeared to fall behind. But after an hour my colleague sat taking a breath on a garden bench with back pain; the other, who had caught up meanwhile, kept spading. One can guess the outcome at the end of the chore. When one observes experienced craftsmen at work, one sees the same thing: they work calmly but steadily and carefully. Such an attitude also produces fruit in spiritual labor. Hendrik Casimir (1909–2000), a physicist, wrote in his beautiful intellectual biography *Het toeval van de werkelijkheid* [The Coincidence of Reality] how he in 1937–38, when he was a guest for a few months at one of the colleges in Cambridge, "discovered the art of working very hard at your leisure." A Benedictine work attitude is related to this, just like the abbot who advised his novices to keep the same attitude in chapel as in recreation: relaxed; and in recreation, the same attitude as in chapel: with dignity. Even with a full agenda one can daily strive to do one's work relaxed and with dignity. The challenge is to keep that attitude of relaxed dignity even when your collection of tasks demands the impossible. In the *Rule*, it appears that this situation was not unfamiliar to Benedict, for it has a chapter entitled "If a Brother Is Commanded to Do Impossible Things" (ch. 68, p. 96):

> If it happens that difficult or impossible tasks are laid on a brother, let him nevertheless receive the order of the one in authority with all meekness and obedience. But if he sees that the weight of the burden altogether exceeds the limit of his strength, let him submit the reasons for his inability to the one who is over him in a quiet way and at an opportune time, without pride, resistance, or contradiction. And if after these representations the Superior still persists in his decision and command, let the subject know that this is for his good, and let him obey out of love, trusting in the help of God.

At first sight we see a text full of goodness and docility that to us is almost intolerable. But here also it is possible to translate Benedict's insights in a way that may be fruitful for us.[3]

---

[3] I owe the exposition that follows to the book of Norvene Vest, *Friend of the Soul: A Benedictine Spirituality of Work,* Boston, 1997, 133–35.

Clearly, this is not about something that is only a bit difficult or problematic, but about a task that appears to lie beyond your strength. Yet, your superior (and sometimes that is you) demands a response to this situation. Our spontaneous answer should be: don't start something or take on something additional that you really can't handle. But Benedict suggests that a totally different response is also possible, to wit a response that can move you further, as it were, in three stadia or levels, beyond a simple "I just cannot do it."

The first step is to answer this impossible-seeming order with a "gentle mind" (thus, without a hard aversion), making the best of it: give it a try. Who knows, we may underestimate what lies in us, and we find ourselves in the happy situation that an attentive abbot, who, after all, needs to see to it that there is something to be desired for the strong, that we are now facing something that heretofore had not been doable. To our surprise we might discover that what was impossible until now can be done.

However, the abbot or we may have wrongly estimated our capabilities and the bar may really appear to be too high. Benedict suggests a course of counseling with the leader. Such counsel requires great care: it should be done at the right moment and in the right manner. This counsel may lead to the liberating insight that the time for this task is not yet ripe; unburdened by frustration, we can then direct our energies to what we are capable of doing. But it can also happen that the situation is such that we will be sent back to the impossible situation (or, we may choose that ourselves), because that chore needs doing and no one else is available to do it.

Then comes an interesting and wise third suggestion: keep listening but not with clamped teeth and contorted willpower, but out of love, trusting in God's help, or, to put it in a secular vein: do it with a smile. Sometimes it happens that precisely in an attitude of "relaxed" and "trustful" recreation we might cross a former boundary. But if it does not succeed or does so only moderately, in that case also, an attitude of relaxed dignity, without sour self-reproach or resentful grumbling at our superior, is the best way of responding to what appears difficult or impossible.

"Bearing Fruit in Season"

The earlier cited book of David Steindl-Rast, *De muziek van de stilte—een dag uit het kloosterleven* [The Music of Silence—A Day in the Monastic Life], very appealingly describes how the various seasons of the monastic day (Matins, Prime, Lauds, Sext, Noon, Vespers, and Compline) each has its own tonality and as it were divide the day into parts. Each of the seasons knows its own fruits. The night watch signifies openness, a sustained waiting on who may come. The day is opened by singing Prime together (often joined with Lauds) in the early morning; it is a moment to order our attitude at the beginning of the work: not to get rid of it as soon as possible, but to see each moment as a chance to give a response from the heart. Of course, that won't succeed for the full 100 percent—it is good and realistic to realize, already at the beginning of the day, that there will be moments of bad listening, and unfaithful and faulty responses. The brief Sext reminds us that at any time during the day we can begin anew. That will be necessary, for the good intentions and the energy of the morning ebb away. It is a good habit to lay down our activities midway through the workday and direct ourselves to orientation points of value. That can give us a new inspiration and straighten our backs, for it is all too tempting to start dawdling and producing half-work, to move along with the "moral gravity" always directed downward; precisely by getting something handed on "from on high" the difficult movement "against gravity" may be stimulated. At noon many of us know a "dip," the "little noon devil": again there is the temptation to leave things be and though we keep busy at the office or elsewhere, we have really gone home already. At that point it is good to take a break, to breathe spiritually one way or another, and then to begin again, though perhaps with the realistic consciousness that your energy is finite and, fortunately, there will be an opportunity tomorrow to respond. Vespers, at the end of the workday, is the moment to take off our work clothes. It is also the moment to be reconciled with tensions and failure of self and others. After Vespers, the day takes on a different color and a different tempo. There is time for reading, for the evening meal together, for recreation. Finally, there is another meeting together to round off the day by singing, in the simple but warm season of the Compline: examination of conscience, prayer for forgiveness, always the same three psalms (4, 91 and 134), the Song of Simeon ("Now let your servant go in peace"), Petitions, Blessing by abbot or prior, and a Hymn of Mary sung in the dark. Then the silence of the night sets in. Actually, it is still rather early to go to sleep, but you read some in the silence of your cell or you write a few lines in your diary. In any event, there are no joint activities anymore and there is no talking. The time before going to sleep is a time of rest and being alone with oneself, till the day is opened together again the following morning, singing (mostly with hoarse and sleepy voices). In my abbey the rhythm of being alone and being together becomes quite visible. At the other seasons of the day and with the celebration of the Eucharist the monks arrange themselves as a *community* in the cloister as they enter the abbey church two by two. At the conclusion of the service, they file out of the abbey church, again two by two. But after the Compline, they leave the chapel one by one, at the moment they choose. And at the early service for readings they also enter one by one, some a bit earlier, others in the nick of time. Between the silence of the night and the early service all are *monachus* (from *monos*, meaning "one," "single," and "solitary"); between Prime and Compline one is also, and above all, *frater* (brother), singing, working, eating, and recreating together.

Naturally, this cannot be imitated or translated very easily to secular life. But it is also good elsewhere to take into account the seasons of the day and with the fact that the fruits of those seasons may differ. It is asking for trouble and mistakes to begin, near the end of the day, with a chore which demands much concentration and energy. It is equally wrong to begin early in the morning, while you are still fresh and energetic, with a very light and silly chore. Yet, it often happens. Quite a few leaders who spend time in their offices begin their workday by checking their mail, reflecting on their first reaction to it, calling a few people on very divergent questions, giving diverse instructions to coworkers of the office. The starting energy of the day is quickly fragmented and dissipated; moreover, psychological investigation points out that what you do first is experienced as the most important, and what one does subsequently is done with a less alert mind. For these reasons, in a Benedictine attitude the approach would be the reverse. Start the workday immediately with that which demands the most attention, concentration, and energy. Keep the mail, responses, and telephone calls for the end of the day (except, of course, if something urgent demands a quick response).

Also marking some moments of the day, translations of the rhythm between Prime and Compline, can help produce the specific color and the unique qualities of the daily seasons better and more fruitfully—provided they are maintained with some stick-to-itiveness. The opportunities for this will differ depending on the situation and the person; however, with some creativity, moments may be provided when you keep silent for a while, turn the lock for five minutes and attentively read a few poems, take a real break and talk with a few brothers and sisters over a cup of soup about everything except the work and the workweek, paying attention to the people around you, etc. Even moments of "play" and "doing nothing" can and must be built in: they are of vital importance for an organization. Yet, they are the first to be let go when we become busy and important or when we are up against it. But just like children stop playing when they are unhappy, afraid, or sick, in the same manner the absence of "play" in an organization (whether it is about a research group, a metal factory, or a diocese), is a certain signal of anxiety, sickness, and unhappiness. Obversely, "play" and "playfulness" are conditions for the practice of human creative functions. There is a direct correlation between play and creativity, between doing nothing and new fruitfulness. An organization which is not functioning well should "play" more to let the creativity of people flourish again. Precisely then it is important to take the "times of recreation" seriously. "Relaxation" and play strengthen commitment and motivation, and stimulate the openness toward the things that renew and refresh.

For those with extra responsibility, it is important to build moments of "being *monachus*" into the rhythm of the day: periods when the door of your room remains closed, not only to keep working, concentrated, and undisturbed, but also for moments of silence and somehow to refuel spiritually. Silence is needed to come into contact with the Spirit, or secularly put: to perform maintenance on a good mentality and condition of your soul. It is not good to be drained constantly; in order to be available responsibly, to be "alone" regularly is a nourishing peripheral condition. Periods of silence are exercises of the internal hearing apparatus; exercising of internal silence is a condition for listening and hospitality. It is certainly true that precisely the people who are quiet and who concentrate are often so clearly *present* that they can subsequently stimulate others to live in a quieter and more concentrated manner.

Such opportunities for the improvement of quality are often the first we let go when we become busy and important: silence and recreation are eliminated as a matter of course; we become noisy and turbulent and with our unrest we affect others. The Benedictine attitude is precisely the reverse. Those who receive extra responsibility need to listen more, like the brother who became prior and then *doubled* his time for daily meditation.

For the rest of the day also, Benedict teaches us a few useful things. It matters indeed how you begin your day and how you end it. It can happen in a sloppy and frayed manner or in a quiet, dignified, and relaxed way. This will color the day and the night one way or another. It is a question of psychic hygiene both to begin the day attentively and beautifully and also to close it attentively and beautifully, so that in the morning we may open our hands to the light, and have peace at night with the things in which we failed and with which we may be content. In each context we may think of small rituals of how we mark beginning, middle, and end, to cultivate the time and let it bear fruit in season.

EPILOGUE

Benedictine Life: Life of One Piece

In this book we have tried to translate a number of aspects of Benedictine life into other contexts in which people live and work together. In this closing paragraph I wish to emphasize [again] that even the smallest details of spirituality are bound together in *unity*. The three quality rules of *stabilitas, conversio,* and *obedientia* together form such a unity of attitudes, bound together and mutually presupposing one another. It is impossible to arrive at lasting change and improvement of quality *(conversio),* or to listen properly to what is demanded of you *(obedientia)* without a sometimes tough, daily commitment *(stabilitas).* You could not maintain the latter if you had not given your "yes" from the heart to the invitation to change your life—even if that happens with much falling and getting up again.

This interrelationship of the rules for quality subsequently expands to *everything,* and not only to the "religious" that we associate with what happens in chapel. In the Benedictine attitude there *are* no nonreligious domains. There *are* no unholy and holy places, there *are* no unholy and holy times and activities. *Everything* needs to be regarded as holy vessels, *everything* is an object for sanctification. Your kitchen gas stove may be your altar, pealing potatoes or folding laundry may be done in the "Benedictine" manner or sloppily and hastily, which is sin. Every place is a place to be sanctified, each moment is a moment to be sanctified. In such an attitude, the maintenance of the garden, the keeping of the books and even a birthday celebration can be sacramental situations, offering chances for *the sacrament of the present moment*. Every place and each situation offer opportunities in one way or another to be a good abbot or a good cellarer.

Benedictine life is literally *simple* in the sense that it is not complicated. It is at the same time very difficult and very easy. The difficulty has to do with the persistence of attention and commitment, with *stabilitas*. The easy part has to do with the fact that we can just begin with it, *wherever we happen to be*, in small things nearby, and each day anew. There are so many opportunities for transformation nearby, for small impulses toward quality, for example, to improve, with small steps, the climate of your (work) environment. And these impulses, no matter how small, often continue to work because everything is related to everything else. Precisely the saying of that brief but good word to your coworker may cause him to be more effective in a situation of consultation hours later, or else, happily come home to his family. Working day by day on your personal integrity, thus to learn to lead a life "of one piece" has far-reaching social consequences. And daily having your "weak coals" fanned into flame by quality sources, can give you sufficient glow-power to stimulate others.

The appeal which the Benedictine lifestyle makes on us "is a direct invitation to our souls to awaken from our defensive cynicism, to choose a different road, to stop chattering, to listen" (David Steindl-Rast). *Ausculta* is the first word of the *Rule*. It is a fruitful attitude for *every* beginning.

General Index

abbot, 32–34
   leadership and the, 1, 47–62
Augustine of Hippo, 38
Aurelius, Marcus, 17
ausculta (obsculta), 15, 27, 57, 75, 88

benedicamus domino, 29, 30
Bingen, Hildegard of.
   See Hildegard of Bingen
Bohr, Niels, x, 49, 69
Buber, Martin, 14, 39, 41, 42

Cary-Elwes, Columba, 11
Celestine Promise, The 6, 12
cellarer *(cellarius)*, 5, 15, 45, 47, 62–69
   fatherhood and the, 62
cheerfulness, 35, 36, 53, 56
contemplatio, 38
conversatio (conversio) morum, 6, 12, 20, 25–27, 30, 31, 39, 43, 51, 57, 71, 75, 77, 79, 87
correctio, 58

De Waal, Esther, 11
decision-making, 31–34
domus Dei, 68, 69

Einstein, Albert, x, 69

glory (praise) of God, ix, x, 6, 8
Gregorian chant, 4
grumbling, 34–35, 56, 60, 76–77
Grün, Anselm, 11, 65, 66

Hildegard of Bingen, 2, 42
Hildegard's Abbey, 1, 2, 4, 5
homo viator, 19
hospitality, 29–31, 85
humilitas, 67

lectio divina, xi, 12, 37–39, 43, 54, 72
Lonergan, Bernard, S.J. 18, 19, 27, 48

meditatio, 38
Murdoch, Iris, 3
murmuratio, 35, 73.
   See also grumbling.

obedientia, 12, 20, 22, 27–29, 39, 87
oblates, 11–12
oratio, 38

parenthood, 48–49
pervenies, 15
Psalm 1, 39–43

radiation of monastic life, 3–4
reading, xi

89